Embrace You

Kathleen M. Peters

DEDICATION

To Ron: You deserve many crowns in heaven. Thank you for always believing in me even when I did not. You are my favorite human.

CONTENTS

ACKNOWLEDGMENTS

It's a strange thing to write a book. At first it feels as though it's all about you and what you will write on a page, but in the end it is quantifiably more than that. This workbook would never have come to life without these key people. Really, it feels as if they wrote it; I just happened to write down some words. It is these beautiful people who made my book a transformational work.

Thank you to all of my Embrace You Test Group members Stacey, Aimee, Megan, Stephanie, Jessica, Kristi, and Connie. Your feedback made this work what it is today. Thank you for your honesty, willingness to be vulnerable, and a devotion to help me make this a useful workbook. I could not have done this without your help.

To my dear friend, Therapist Connie: From day one you encouraged and supported this dream. I'll never forget that warm Spring afternoon sitting on your back deck as you read the beginnings of this manuscript. It was that day I knew this might be a helpful tool for women. Thank you for helping with the intricacies of writing the Embrace You Group Safety Guidelines, and Empathy and Traumatic Story Responses. Thanks for all the times you offered business advice as well as a strong empathetic shoulder to cry on, but most of all thank you for the times you gently reminded me that not all my *shoulds* deserve a long and full life.

Thank you to the women of Straight Up Real Mamas. It was in you that this workbook found life and I discovered my purpose. You taught me why empathy is vital to creating an authentic environment, how being real can free women from the prison of attempting to be perfect, and the immense power that "I am not alone" holds. We have laughed together and cried together. I am so very grateful to all of you.

To Megan Payne my beautiful artistic friend: Thank you for the amazing illustrations you created for the workbook. I can't wait for the second revision to show them off.

To Angela Carhart my incredibly resourceful friend: Thank you for writing the Resource page for women who have trauma as a part of their story. That was a piece I wanted done well and it was. And thank you for your encouraging words, "…you've really got something special here," after viewing the raw manuscript. You will never know how much that fueled me to keep moving forward.

To Kelly Bentz my therapist: Thank you for walking with me through my painful memories and reminding me I can find healing. Thank you for cheering me on in my business and your willingness to read the rough draft of this manuscript.

To Ron Peters, my husband, my best friend, my business partner, and technology superhero: After 24 years of marriage, you've gotten to be an expert in my tell-tale I-can't-do-this-I-want-to-give-up signs. At each point, especially anything having to do with technology, you swooped in with your reassuring words and hopeful encouragement and made me believe this would be no big deal. In looking back at the whole process now, that was a pretty fantastic trick because it *was* a BIG deal! In so many ways, this is your workbook. You took my scrambling of words and made it readable. Thank you, sweet man.

KATHLEEN M. PETERS

INTRODUCTION

"Real is what happens when you become your true self – not a contrived, shiny, pretend thing – and are loved despite, and maybe even because of your imperfections."
- Toni Raiten-D'Antonio, "The Velveteen Principles"

Dear Reader,

I am so glad you picked up this little workbook because it means you are open to exploring who God made you to be. It means you may be ready to embrace that beautiful woman who shares your same beating heart; that woman who God made amazing. Yes, I'm talking about you. My hope is that even if now you can't quite visualize this woman I speak of, by the end of this workbook, you will have a tiny peek into the real woman God knit together in her mother's womb.

How do you know if this book is for you?

If you've found yourself thinking:

- Being real sounds wonderful, but I don't even know who my real self is.
- I want to discover who I am. I want to be in touch with this person God made me to be, but I don't know how or where to start.
- I want to learn more about how God made me.

- I want to learn to celebrate who I am and who I am not as one beautiful package.

If this is you, friend, I believe you've come to the right place to begin your journey. In this little workbook you will find 20 questions that are intended to help you dig deep into not only discovering who you are, but also help you begin to embrace all of you.

How This Book Came to Be

In March of 2016, I set out on what seemed to be a small adventure. You know, a weekend trip of sorts; the only-pack-2-pairs-of-underwear type. I created what I thought would be a small Facebook group for moms with fifty or so women. Why the number fifty? To be honest, I thought I only knew that many.

Why would I do such a thing?

As I had begun to unpack the real me (she was buried deeply under all the things she thought she should be), the one with gifts, passions, and struggles, I came to realize God had made me on purpose. He had made me, Kathleen Peters, the way he did because he had a plan to use me to do certain things. I heard his voice calling me to be that beautiful imperfect girl; the one who was a mixed bag of beauty, light, dark, and struggle. He wanted it all because he had stuff for me to do.

God began to gently whisper to me, "Sweet girl, I love you just the way you are. If you will embrace all of you (the beauty and the struggle), I will show you the ridiculously fun and outrageous things I have perfectly designed you to do. And girl, you are going to love it!"

It was mind blowing really.

I say I unpacked the real me because it was always there; I just didn't recognize it or place any real value on it. I began to see that reaching out and encouraging women could be one of God's purposes for my life.

One of my loves is to encourage women in their role as mom and I have found myself in countless situations doing just that; it became a running theme in my life. I found this to be a running theme in my life.

As I connected with moms, it seemed that too often I would hear her say things like, "I know I shouldn't feel that way about my kids, husband, other women, cooking, cleaning, my role as a stay-at-home mom, my role as a work outside the home mom." The women traveling across my path were unsure they were pulling off this mom gig. Most of them were pretty sure they were totally screwing up their kids or just plain failing. Most were struggling with feelings of inadequacies as they compared themselves to the mom they felt they *should* be.

And so, I set out to create a place on Facebook for moms to come for encouragement. I wanted a place where they could be free to be honest about the struggles of being a mom, friend, and human being without fear of being judged or criticized.

My dream was for the Christian woman to be able to lay down all the shoulds she was carrying around and simply be real about what life was really like in her home. I sensed that the Christian mom not only had all the lifestyle mommy wars to deal with, but she also had a whole slew of shoulds that come with being a Christian woman.

She worried if her kids didn't memorize scripture, read the bible on their own, have their own personal quiet time, or didn't want to go to church. She was not only responsible for raising upstanding citizens, but also for making sure their salvation was secure. It's a heavy load this mom lugs around and this doesn't even account for all the negative messages she is transporting from her own upbringing.

God gave me a tender heart for this mom. I knew there was power in what my friend Jessica calls, "Me too!" You know when you are struggling and another woman says, "Oh, yeah!! Me too. I've felt that way before." There is something freeing and reassuring when you discover you aren't the only one. As my good friend Misty says, "You mean I'm not a freak of nature after all? What a relief!"

This is how my Facebook group Straight Up Real Mamas came to be birthed. I wanted women to find freedom, peace, Me-Too-Friends, and encouragement to face another day in the battles to be a good mom, Christian, friend, and human being.

I opened the doors on my group, invited some friends, and in a matter of 24 hours, there were 120 plus women in the group sharing, encouraging, and posting pictures of cluttered closets and messy kitchens. "Um. What just happened?" I was overwhelmed by the obvious need for women to freely share in a safe environment.

That's how I walked smack dab into my purpose. It was exhilarating.

As the group began to grow, I posted questions that would help us get to know one another better but my ulterior motive was to guide women to this place of letting herself off the hook for not being all things to all people. My deep desire was that each woman would not only see she was not alone in her struggle to keep afloat with all the expectations society, her church, her current family and family of origin placed on her, but also that she was okay just the way she was.

And those questions are now what you hold in your own hands.

You see, I believe, buried deeply under all your shoulds, is the woman God desires you to embrace. The way he made you is for a reason. I believe as you sift through all the things that make you unique (as well as those that make you the same), as you face your imperfections, struggles, and even the things about being a woman that drive you to the brink of freefall, you will begin to find her. And this is point of Embrace You.

What Can Get in Our Way - Lies We Believe

Please be aware there may be lies you believe about yourself that could get in the way on your excursion to embracing you. It's important to take note of these untruths as they can keep you from becoming the woman God designed you to be.

1. Lies From Our Family of Origin

You may have been told you were fat, too thin, stupid, too smart for your own good, uncoordinated, too serious, too loud, too quiet, or any number of other lies. Whether your family members gave you those messages with spoken words or were implied, many of us have carried these misrepresentations into our adult lives. For some of us, it doesn't matter what the scales says, we will always be too fat because a family member told us that as a child.

2. Lies From Our Education

What you experienced in school can carry heavy baggage for you as an adult. Maybe you struggled in a certain subject and believe to this day you are "bad" in that area. Or maybe your art project was made fun of and to this day you believe you are not creative.

3. Lies From our Enemy

I believe our enemy, Satan, has it out for you. The Bible says he roams the earth like a hungry lion waiting to devour you[1]. If you're a Jesus-girl, you are not only disliked by this guy, you are hated. Why? Guilt by association. You see, Satan despises God. And so, as God's kiddo yourself, you too are his enemy.

One thing that has been pivotal in my growth as a human being is recognizing the intent of the enemy. His goal isn't necessarily to get me to do bad stuff, (although, I'm sure that's pretty satisfying for him), but his main course of action is to paralyze me. How does he accomplish this? By reminding me of the lies I already believe about the character of God, the world, and myself. When I believe, "I'm not _____ enough to _____," fear keeps me from moving forward in that direction. The very thing God was jumping up and down excited for me to do with the gifts he gave me remains undone. Fear sets in and I become ineffective. All because of some lies. There is a reason Jesus called the enemy the Father of lies[2].

It is because of these lies that the workbook questions are designed to take a close look at what you truly believe. When you identify the junk in your beliefs and hold it up to the truth, you can begin to reveal the real you.

---

[1] 1 Peter 5:8
[2] John 8:44

HOW TO USE EMBRACE YOU

Each of the 20 questions in <u>Embrace You</u> have their own page for writing your responses. Please feel free to answer these in the way that feels most comfortable to you. Some women will want to get their own empty journal to write in a free writing style. Others will write out lists in bullet form, while others will want to draw pictures or use colored pens.

You may have difficulties deciding which format you'll use to record your answers. My recommendation is to pick a question and start writing in the workbook. If that doesn't feel right, try something else. It may take a few questions to get a feel for what would be most enjoyable.

Where?

I recommend you find a comfortable space to work on your questions. This could be at a café or on your own living room couch with a soft blanket. Whatever you choose, make it somewhere you can concentrate.

How much time should I give myself?

In our test Embrace You Groups (small groups of women who shared their workbook answers with one another), most women said they wished they had given themselves more time to reflect and ponder each question. Most questions can be answered in as little as 15 to 30 minutes, but to get the most out of them, I suggest choosing a question and then taking the next week to think it over before writing your answer.

How Quickly?

You are the Captain of this Ship. This is your journey to uncover and embrace you, and I hereby dub you the Grand Poohbah of this process. That's right, you get to decide what questions to answer and in what order. You can give yourself full permission to even skip questions. GASP!! I know. It's crazy.

That also means you get to choose the speed of this ship. Maybe you answer a question a week. Or maybe you are ready to attack it with a vengeance by answering one a day. You decide. Be patient with yourself. Sometimes, the epiphanies take time. Sigh. I know. It can be frustrating.

Need a little extra help?

One of my biggest beefs with workbooks or Bible studies has been with the lack of clarity in the questions asked. It's frustrating to me especially since I want to get the most out of the study. Side note: this *may* have something to do with my need to get all the answers right. Yes, I'm a Recovering Perfectionist.

So after each question, I've included "Kathleen's Thoughts" to shed a bit of light on why this question is in the workbook and to give you a feel for what I'm hoping you might discover about yourself.

I want warn you though, the beauty of <u>Embrace You</u> is that there are no right or wrong answers. You alone hold the answer key, my friend. You get to decide how you want interpret each question. If you answer a question, read Kathleen's Thoughts, and realize that was not the direction I seemed to be leading, I want to assure you, you have *not* answered incorrectly. This workbook is about you, not me.

The Dangers of "Kathleen's Thoughts"

For some of us, it will be excruciatingly tempting to read "Kathleen's Thoughts" first before allowing ourselves to ruminate on our own answer. This would be me. The danger though would be that you would forget to trust yourself that you have your own answer and that is the whole point of Embrace You (you discovering who you are).

So my friend, have faith in yourself, and do your best to write down your primary thoughts and be wary of the temptation to respond how you think you should. This just gets in the way of unearthing the real woman we're trying to reach. Whatever your answers are, they will give you a view of who you really are. And *that* is what we're after.

Take it to the next level: Embrace You Groups

"Bring your brokenness, and I'll bring mine
'Cause love can heal what hurt divides
And mercy's waiting on the other side
If we're honest"
-Francesca Battistelli

As you begin this process of embracing you, my hope is you would then begin to feel the courage to little by little take that woman out of the box and show her to the world. I know that can be scary so I've created a structure for you that could assist you with the first baby steps – Embrace You Groups.

Embrace You Group: A small group of women who want to practice vulnerability with one another by sharing their answers to Embrace You.

In the next chapter (Embrace You Groups), I walk you through starting a small (2-6 women) Embrace You Group (EYG) using the questions from this book. This intimate group could be a great way to flex your vulnerability muscles in a safe environment.

How Embrace You Groups (EYG) Came to Be

Saying our goodbyes for the night, the four of us embrace. This has been a special night. There is a warmth and a tenderness present unlike any I've experienced in a small group. I feel incredibly close to each one even though mere months ago, I would've described each as simply a "casual friend".

By the length of the hugs, it's clear I am not the only one. I find myself close to tears as one woman expresses exactly how I feel, "I can't even tell you how refreshing it is to be able to just be real with you guys. It feels so good to be with other women and not have to be on guard. I feel like I can be honest with you and you won't judge me. I know you love me and accept me. It's such a beautiful thing."

As I walk to my car, this overwhelming burden envelops me. "I want this for every woman! Every women deserves to experience this."

And yet I know in the last 2 months each of us in that small group had to fight past our own fears to get here. The four of us know what brought us to this moment.

Courage. Empathy.

The formula was to have courage to show our own underbelly (those tender places each of us keep well-hidden for fear of how we'll be perceived) and then to withhold judgment by the other members coupled with a generous dose of affirmation and empathy.

Vulnerability (showing our underbellies) can be exceedingly frightening, but research tells us it's essential if deep connection is to be accomplished. And deep connection is what many of us are not experiencing in our friendships, but desperately want. More and more of us are feeling lonely despite our increased availability through social media. But then social media is not the place where you generally find an abundance of vulnerability and empathy.

What I've found is that though bringing our true self (the honest, authentic version) to the table can be truly daunting, the rewards can far outweigh the fear. When our real self is revealed in the safety of accepting loving people, God can use that situation to free us. I believe he is waiting to unburden us from the lies we've been taught, chosen to believe, or had spoken over us. Yes. He wants us free and unburdened. His yoke is easy. His burden is light.

In this little study group of four women, I got a front row seat to this magnificent unburdening. Together we identified things from our childhood that had contributed to lies we'd believed about ourselves, and how healthy relationships work.

There were moments I felt surprised, almost shocked at their stories because I couldn't believe the precious women sitting across the couch from me not only endured such terrible childhood experiences, but that she was also this amazingly gifted, well put together woman in spite of them. Other times, I wanted to scream, "NO!!! That isn't fair. No! That isn't true!" But I chose to allow my sweet friend to simply share.

We nodded as she spoke. We listened deeply in the parts of our hearts that we didn't even know existed. I found myself wishing I could go back in time and grab that little girl (my sweet friend) and tell her how amazing she is and that what is happening to her little self is not right, and not to believe the lies she is being told. I wanted to hug this small child because if I could only go back in time and hold her and speak truth into her, the grown woman sitting next to me would be different.

Not that I want her to be different at the core of who she is because I am already amazed at her beauty, but that I want her to see what I see. I want her to believe the truth about herself.

This is my hope for you, friend, that you would see the truth about yourself. And sometimes it's easier to see that truth when you are surrounded by those willing to meet you in that soft underbelly place without judgment.

In a Group or With a Friend

You'll notice every workbook question has a section, "In a Group or With a Friend." When you are ready to move to that next level, this will be your guide. And again, you get to be the captain of this ship; you decide how often and where to meet, which questions you will discuss, and who you will invite.

Since an Embrace You Group is meant to provide a place for you to practice being vulnerable, you will want to pay close attention to *who* you invite. The trick is they must be with women you feel safe.

EMBRACE YOU GROUPS

Embrace You Groups (EYGs)

Okay, so you love the idea of asking a few women to join you on this journey of discovering the real you. Hooray! Do you know how incredibly brave you are for even *thinking* about getting vulnerable with other women? Yep, it's true. There is courage rumbling around in your heart, friend.

Because vulnerability involves risk for everyone involved, this chapter is a compilation of things I would love for you to consider before taking the leap.

Inviting Women

The purpose of an EYG is to provide a safe place for women to explore who they really are, as well as empathize, encourage, and affirm the other women in the group as they do the same. This is your cheering squad, your confidants. I call them Heart Holders (see **Identifying Heart Holders** in the Appendix).

What are Heart Holders?

These are women who will believe the best about you, seek first to understand, listen with their hearts, and never judge or criticize you. When you are with these women, you feel seen, heard, and valued.

Sounds awesome, huh?

In order to achieve this bit of heaven, you will want to carefully go through **Identifying Heart Holders** to make sure you are only inviting true heart holders. Trust me on this. As tempting as it will be to send out a mass Facebook post to all your friends to see who is interested in joining your group...

Don't do it!

We're looking for the care and safety of everyone involved, and not all women are up to the task. We all have a friend we love, but would never share our deepest fears. We know instinctively that this woman would stomp all over our heart (with the best of intentions, of course). This is what we want to avoid.

"I Can't Wait to Help My Introvert Friends Be More Real!"

If you already love being real and are not afraid of saying things others may be hesitant to say, it might be tempting to gather all your friends who aren't that way and form an EYG. This may seem like the perfect opportunity to push the quieter ones out of their shell. After all, it's more fun to be vulnerable when others around are you willing to jump in too.

I would ask that instead you would align yourself with others like you. Or be willing to be very quiet in your group to give space and time to the more timid. Those of us bolder ones who are comfortable sharing our real selves to anyone who will listen can create a frightening atmosphere to those who don't yet feel as free to be real. In our excitement we can unknowingly and unintentionally add pressure. If you want your EYG to be successful, pressure can never be a part of the equation.

"I Know Exactly Who Needs to Be More Real!"

Embrace You Groups (EYG) are meant to provide a safe place for the woman who is *ready* to share. If you start this venture with the intention of pushing a woman into being in your group because she needs it, you'll want to reconsider.

It is better to stick with what *you* want and need, and then look for friends who want the same thing. If you want to forge deeper friendships through vulnerability, then look for women who are seeking the same. High pressure sales to a woman not ready to be vulnerable can only spell disaster for the future of your group.

"I Can't Wait to Invite My Friends! I Just Know They'll Want to Join me."

I know you're excited. Me too. Here's the thing: you want to keep this low pressure. It's imperative that women feel they can say no. Trust me, you do not want a woman in your group who felt pressured into coming. She will either struggle to be vulnerable, have trouble attending regularly (she won't feel committed to the group), or not adhere to the Safety Guidelines, all of which will make your group suffer in the end.

You want women who are just as excited as you. And if that means only one friend attends, it will be far better than five who aren't really into it.

"My Friend is Hesitant to Participate. What do I do?"

That's good she's voicing her hesitancy. You want your members to be honest. This is a good sign she might fit right in.

If she's truly interested, my suggestion is to encourage her to read over "**Process of Choosing Members**" and "**EYG Safety Guidelines Agreement**" found below and at:

http://kathleenmpeters.com/embrace-you-groups-safety-guidelines/.

She could also get a copy of the workbook and try out some of the questions on her own. This will give her a chance to see if she's ready for this level of vulnerability in a group setting. Then tell her you'll get back to her in a couple of weeks to find out if she's ready to jump in.

Process of Choosing Your EYG Members

Choosing Your First EYG Member

1. Read "**Identifying Heart Holders**" (HH) found in the Appendix. You want to invite women from the left column.

2. Make a list of your Heart Holders.

3. Choose one of your favorite Heart Holders and invite her.

4. Ask her to read through the **EYG Safety Guidelines Agreement** and sign if she agrees. By signing the agreement, a woman is noting the seriousness of this group and the importance of sticking to the guidelines to maintain safety. If a woman knows everyone in the group is signing this document, she can feel more assured these guidelines will be adhered to by the entire group.

Choosing Your Subsequent Members

1. New member makes her Heart Holder (HH) list.

2. Discuss with new member who you both know on each other's lists.

Q: What if we don't have any of the same names on our lists? What do we do next?

A: Take her top choice and walk together through the Identifying Heart Holders questions. Do you feel assured this potential new member firmly fits in the "Gravitate Towards" column?

If possible and not awkward, see if you could meet her HH in a neutral setting, such as a coffee shop or friend gathering. It would be best if her HH doesn't know she's being interviewed for the position. You could then see how you feel around her in person.

Q: What if we walk through the "Gravitate Towards" column and I'm still uncomfortable with her choice?

A: You get to say, "Yeah, that's not feeling like a comfortable choice for me. Who would be another great HH?" Appeasing your friend because you don't want to hurt her feelings can be a deadly formula for your group. If you feel discomfort with her choice now, it may effect what you will and will not share later. Take good care of you now.

3. Repeat Steps 1-2 of Process of Choosing the New Members until you have your EYG. The ideal would be 2-5 women total. 6 maximum. Larger groups require too much time for each woman to share.

EYG Safety Guidelines Agreement

Because of the nature of Embrace You (women becoming vulnerable and authentic with other women), it is imperative the group is a safe place to share. Not every woman may be ready or able at this time in her life.

1. Each potential new member will read the following guidelines *before* agreeing to participate in the Embrace You Group (EYG). If they agree with the entirety of the document, they should sign and return to the person who invited them.

2. Each new member agrees to read the instructions Process of Choosing New Members before inviting their own Heart Holders. All potential new members must first be discussed with all existing group members and agreed on together.

IMPORTANT: Please *do not* invite a girlfriend without first discussing with the other participants.

I, _____ agree to the following:

Freedom

    A. I do not have to share any of my answers from the workbook. I can share as little or as much as I'm comfortable. When I don't want to share, I will respond with "I'll pass this time." It is agreed that I will not need to provide an explanation of why.

    B. If a member chooses to pass on a question, I will not ask for more information. I will not ask, "Why?" or even say, "Too hard to share today?" I will nod with a compassionate smile.

Brevity

    C. For the sake of the health of the group and to make sure each participant gets a chance to share, I agree to set my phone's timer for 5 minutes when it's my turn to speak. When my time is up, I agree to allow the next member to share. I am welcome to finish my story another time (on the phone, or over coffee with a friend).

Appropriate Responses to Trauma Stories

    D. When a member shares a particularly tough story (it involves trauma, abuse, grief), I will respond from one of the **Empathy and Traumatic Story Responses** (see Appendix)

Inviting Friends

    E. I will respect each member's need for safety and will not invite a friend to the group without first talking with the other members.

Confidentiality

F. I will respect each member's privacy and keep anything shared confidential. I won't even share with my husband or kids. I am free to share my own responses to the workbook questions with anyone I wish.

Attendance

G. Understanding my absence significantly changes the dynamics of such a small group, I commit to attend each group meeting, come on time, and stay to the end.

H. If due to illness I cannot attend, **I will text all members** and they can decide if they would still like to meet.

Participation

I. I agree this is a place of sharing and encouragement. If I find myself needing to convince another member to my way of thinking, I will stop, take a deep breath and say, "I apologize. I just realized I was trying to tell you what to do. I'm going to stop now."

J. I agree to stay away from *should* statements. For example, you should do this _____.

K. I agree to not bring in others (experts, authors, therapists) into our conversations. "You know, experts say…." I will stick with I-statements, "Here's what I've experienced…" or "I've been learning…"

L. I agree to not give advice unless I am explicitly asked for it.

M. I agree that to be a part of this group I will participate, share, and engage with the group. I may choose to not answer certain questions, but I agree that I will participate.

N. I agree to quickly remove myself from the group if I discover I am not ready to share at this level of vulnerability.

O. I agree to *not* tell members how to feel, "You should feel this way," or "Don't feel that way."

_____   _____
Signature   Date

Is it Necessary Each Member Sign the Safety Guidelines?

Yes! I know for some this may seem to be too restrictive. Please let me assure you of how important this is. You don't want to skip this part of the agreement.

Do you know why most of us choose to not be vulnerable with others? We are afraid we will be rejected, judged or criticized. If we know there is a possibility of that happening, we won't allow ourselves to be exposed to it. It would be like walking into a hungry bear's cave with no protection. Who wants to be eaten alive? No, thank you.

Women in your group need to feel they are in a safe environment to be vulnerable. If there isn't a set understanding that you will all adhere to these guidelines, you will find the depth of your group to be quite shallow.

At my Let's Get Real, Sister! retreats, women love that from the stage I give permission to every participant to share as little or as much as she is comfortable. I then ask the entire group to verbally promise me they will not pressure each other to contribute. This sets the tone of the group that there will be safety.

Another important reason to have group participants sign the **EYG Safety Guidelines** is if a member of your group goes *rogue* and begins to belittle a member for "feeling that way" or slips into giving advice when empathy is needed, the group has a way to course correct. You can then stop and revisit these Guidelines that you all agreed to follow. If necessary, you could also pull that woman aside and remind her of what she signed..

If you do not course correct, the intimacy and vulnerability of the group will be lost. We have all learned from a young age to watch what happens to others who choose to be brave. If the brave person is made to feel small, then the rest of the group knows what will happen to them. In our case, authenticity will be lost and the EYG group will cease to be effective.

How Does the Group Course Correct?

First, you will want to appoint someone in the group as your Facilitator. The Facilitator will agree to keep an eye on a timer and keep the group moving forward through your meeting time. Most likely this will be the woman who formed the group, but feel free to choose someone else who may be more comfortable with keeping the group on track.

If at any time it looks like the group is becoming a counseling session (members are giving each other advice), a place to only complain, or someone is being criticized, the Facilitator will need to direct the group back to the **EYG Safety Guidelines Agreement** and read it aloud.

It may be good to say something like, "Okay, I think maybe we've slipped into that counseling mode that Kathleen says we want to avoid. I'm going to read that section in the Safety Guidelines."

Another situation may be after someone has shared something traumatic, and you are nervous the members will struggle to follow the **Empathy and Traumatic Story Responses**, you could say, "Since, we're all pretty new to this, I just want to take a moment to pause before we respond to _____'s answer. I'd love for us all to turn **Empathy and Traumatic Story Responses** (see Appendix) and follow along while I read.

If a member consistently is not following the Safety Guidelines Agreement, it is imperative for the health of the group that the Facilitator takes that woman aside and reminds her of the Agreement she signed. "How are you feeling about the group? I've been noticing that not giving advice after a woman has shared is a real struggle for you. I know it's really difficult for me too. Here's the thing though, the Safety Guidelines we all signed says we won't give advice. So I'm wondering if you are feeling like this isn't a good fit for you right now. Or if there is a way I can help you to not do that."

Fortunately in our Embrace You Test Groups, we never did need to course correct. If you follow **Process of Choosing Your EYG Members**, make sure each member is not pressured to be in your group, and have each member sign the **EYG Safety Guidelines**, my hope is you will never have to course correct either.

EGY Meetings

Each meeting will consist of 3 agenda items:
- Social Time/Announcements
- Sharing (and responses to sharing)
- Next Meeting Assignment

Meeting Length

2 women = 60 minutes
4 women = 90 minutes

Because each woman is given 5 minutes to share and the group is given 3 minutes to respond, you'll want to plan at least 8 minutes per question per person, plus at least 30 minutes for socializing and announcements.

For example:
4 women x 8 minutes = 32 minutes per question
32 minutes x 2 questions = 64 minutes
64 minutes + 30 minutes Social/Announcements = 94 minutes

Groups of 2

If would like more than 8 minutes for sharing, please feel free to increase your meeting time.

Groups of 6

I recommend you choose 1 Question per meeting to keep your

meeting under 2 hours.

Other sized groups will adjust their times as appropriate.

Sample of First EYG Meetings

Prior to Your First Meeting

- Notify members of the first week's Question assignment (choose only one for the first week)

WEEK 1

Social Time/Announcements:

- Introductions & share phone numbers
- Read aloud both **EYG Group Safety Guidelines** and **Empathy and Appropriate Responses to Trauma Stories**
  - Point out that you can talk to a spouse, close girlfriend, or counselor if you find yourself reeling from another's trauma story. You must keep her identity hidden though.

Sharing:

- Question #1

Members have 5 minutes to share their answer. Give the group 3 minutes to respond before proceeding to the next member's sharing.

Next Meeting Assignment:

- Next Meeting June 6th, 5:30pm, Sarah's house
- Next Week's Questions: #2 and #3

WEEK 2

Social Time/Announcements:

- Point out **Abuse Resources** and **Self-Care** (see Appendix) pages

Sharing:

- Question #2
- Question #3

Next Meeting Assignment:

- Next Meeting June 13th, 5:30pm, Sarah's house
- Next Week's Questions: #3 and #5
- Read **Self-Care** and choose 1 way you will practice self-care in the following weeks.

NOTE:

In our Embrace You Test Groups, participants found it best when we read aloud the questions for the following week at the end of each gathering. This gave women a chance to spend a few days pondering the question before sitting down to write her answers. There were also quite a few women who said they wished they had given themselves more time to work on the question before the meeting. Please make sure to let women know they will want to devote at least 30 minutes to an hour each week to writing their answers.

EMBRACE YOU

QUESTIONS

KATHLEEN M. PETERS

Question 1:

Make a list of things that you love and/or make you happy.

Need some ideas to get started?
Boysenberry pie, the smell of warm pine needles, sand between my toes, peonies, journaling, hiking

Challenge: Get creative! Get out your colored pens or pencils and make a 2 page spread with pictures representing each of your loves. Or write each word in a different color or style of writing. And then share with the rest of us Embrace You women. Take a picture and share on Facebook or Instagram with #thingsilove #embraceyou.

Question 1: Kathleen's Thoughts

God made you unique and sometimes that is most evident when we examine the things we love. It says volumes about who we are.

The year was 1992, I had broken off my engagement and discovered I had been knee deep in a codependent abusive relationship. My new therapist gave me this question as my first homework assignment. At the time, I didn't understand how it could aid in my quest to recover my lost self. It seemed like a silly exercise; a waste of time really. But dear friend, it was a lifeline. I needed to see I was separate from this young man. I needed to see I was unique. It felt as if God were reminding me he made me special on purpose, and he loved me just the way I was. That was the day I began my journey to embrace this women God made.

As my friend, Connie (mental health therapist) keeps reminding me, we are all a spectrum of beauty and storm, light and dark. Unfortunately, I have noticed my focus tends to stay firmly on one particular side of that spectrum, and it ain't on the beauty end, which is unfair. I am a whole package. And so are you. If we only focus on the work to be done, we miss out on the beauty God made. You are the whole package, friend. Please spend some time to take stock of your own beauty. What gives you pure delight? You see, what you love is an integral part of what makes you who you are.

In our Embrace You Test Groups, some women got creative when answering this question. One woman drew picture depictions of the things she loved. Another used colored pens to write out the words in different kinds of lettering. So, if you are feeling creative, get out your colored pens and stickers and try making a 2-page spread in a journal or notebook that shows off your list. Then the next time you struggle to remember who you are, these pages can be your reminder. You may also want to leave some space on a page to add newly discovered loves later.

In a Group or with a Friend

As you go around the room to share, take note of how different and the same other's answers are from your own.

Does it seem strange that your friends don't have the same loves as you?

Please expect this may be a tough question for some women. In many circles, Christian women are discouraged from thinking too much about themselves. This is an attempt, I believe, to keep us from becoming selfish and proud. The end result unfortunately is we don't allow ourselves to even ponder the unique beauty God placed within us.

If there is a woman in your group who struggles with this question, please encourage her to keep at it; she can continue to add to it as she remembers other things that bring her delight.

NOTE: You may want to assign Questions 1 and 2 together.

Group Challenge:

Make a note about your friend's loves and then at some point in the future surprise her with one of them.

Question 2:

Go back to Question 1 (Things that you love). Do you
see a running theme in your list? What do you see?

Question 2: Kathleen's Thoughts

This question digs a bit deeper in helping you discover what it is that recharges you. When you are depleted, at the end of your rope, or exhausted, what would help you to find some respite? Some rest. Maybe even a reset.

In my initial 'Things I Love' List, I noticed there was a theme: I enjoyed them while alone and most had to do with something warm. Going to a party or skiing with friends would not be a recharging event for me. Curling up next to a warm fire, a good book, and a warm beverage would hit the spot.

Don't find a theme in your Love List? No problem. There might not be one.

In a Group or with a Friend

Some women will not find a theme in their list. Please make sure to remind them that it's okay. There might not be one.

It could be fun as a group to look for themes in each other's lists.

Question 3:

What's a dream you've tucked away in your heart in the 'someday' category?

Question 3: Kathleen's Thoughts

The point in asking this question is two-fold.

First is to remind you that outside your many roles as a woman is a person who has dreams.

The second is not to lament unmet dreams, but to give you an opportunity to open up that 'someday box' and remind yourself you have passions.

Dreams, I believe, are placed in us by God and are evidence that he made us on purpose. Not everyone has your dream. As a matter of fact, you would be hard pressed to find someone who held your exact same dream. They might have some of the same details as yours, but they will never have your same life experience, story, and feelings. Your dream is unique and it is part of what makes you who you are.

In a Group or with a Friend

This is a compassion building exercise. Something beautiful happens when women can see into the recesses of each other's hearts, and view her passions and dreams. Women begin to not only root for and respect one another, but often they look for ways to encourage each other to realize their dreams. It's like a tiny window into the woman God made.

Question 4:

If you could write a note to your younger self (from 5 years ago) what would you say?

Question 4: Kathleen's Thoughts

This question provides a chance to reflect on how far you've come and what you've learned. When we tried this question in my Facebook group, I noticed women were not only sweet and gentle with their young selves, but they began to see they were stronger than they had originally thought.

My hope is you will apply the same wisdom you offer your younger-self to your present-self. If your letter advises, "It will all work out. You don't have to worry so much," perhaps this may give you the strength to fight today's trial.

Just as God asked the Israelites to build alters so their children would be reminded of how their ancestors struggled and survived with God walking them through it, I believe this could be an alter making exercise for you.

"If today is a hard day, we would like to gently remind you that your success rate for surviving hard days is 100 percent. You have a perfect record of surviving. You have never not survived a hard day. You rock star. You've got this."
-Laura Parrott-Perry, Say It Survivor[3]

In a Group or with a Friend

You can discuss this question a few ways.

1. Read your letters to each other
2. Give the highlights of your letter
3. Share the advice you gave yourself (if you did)

---

[3] Sayitsurvivor.com is a website providing a platform for survivors of child sexual abuse to tell their stories anonymously.

Question 5:

Do you struggle with self-care? What do you think contributes to this?

Question 5: Kathleen's Thoughts

<u>Self-Care</u>: Taking time out of regular responsibilities of life to focus on you, with the intent to recharge and refresh.

Are there lies you believe about taking care of you? Do you believe it's selfish or that your job is to put everyone else first at all times? Even though Jesus wasn't a mom, he did take care of a lot of people. As a mom myself, I often became overwhelmed with the "Mom! Mom! Mom!" that came from the little people who seemed to be touching me every single minute of the day. Take a deep breath, Kathleen.

I can't imagine what it must have been like for Jesus. Everywhere he went, the crowds seemed to find and surround him; each hoping for his attention and care. Did he ever find the need to escape and take care of himself? Evidence shows us he took time in the early morning and into the night to pray while the crowds were away.[4] Was there something sacred about the timing of those prayers? I think not.

Possibly this was the only time he could be assured to be alone to get recharged and prepared for another hectic day. God designed you, precious lady, to *need* to steal away and do the same. And to reassure the non-morning people, it doesn't have to be at sunrise.

We can only deny ourselves for so long before we become grumpy and resentful (as much as we may attempt to be grateful for every moment we are living). You were designed to need rest.

Funny thing is, God knew some of us might resist taking time to recharge. Go figure. Hmmm. If you are struggling to let yourself take time out for you, I hope you would remind yourself there may have been a very good reason God called for a Sabbath in the 10 Commandments. I don't know. It may just be me.

---

[4] Matthew 14:23; Mark 1:35; Luke 6:12

In a Group or with a Friend

This exercise may bring out the need to tell each other to not feel a certain way. If a woman admits she does not feel she's worthy of self-care, please refrain from telling her she should not feel that way. It's counterproductive and hurtful to have someone tell you how to feel. It may be best to warn the group of this prior to sharing, and then refer everyone to **Empathy and Traumatic Story Responses** (see Appendix).

Here's a challenge using Questions 4 and 5:

Using your list from Question 5, everyone in the group agrees to do something for their own self-care in the next week, and then report back to the group how it went.

Ask yourself while you are doing something to refresh you: Do I feel guilty? If so, what thoughts am I having that are producing that guilt? What do I believe that makes it not okay for me to relax?

NOTE: If your batteries are completely depleted because it's been a long time since you took some time for you, this challenge may not create a feeling of being recharged. Don't give up. It may take many more self-care acts to feel different.

Question 6:

What do you do to help yourself feel refreshed (self-care)? If given a whole day to yourself to recharge, what would you do?

Question 6: Kathleen's Thoughts

See Kathleen's thoughts from Question 5.

In a Group or with a Friend

See Kathleen's thoughts from Question 5.

Question 7:

List your strengths in each of these categories:

- Relational/Social
- Career
- Mental
- Personality
- Aptitude
- Physical

In each category, which of your strengths do you value most?

Challenge: Make a list of your shortcomings. Are any of these also a strength?

KATHLEEN M. PETERS

Question 7: Kathleen's Thoughts

Finding the real you is about discovering how you were made by God. He chose to make you exactly who you are with strengths and struggles.

Picture Him in your kitchen standing over a steaming pot. There is a delicious aroma penetrating the entire room and inviting you in like a warm blanket on a cold day. He tells you He is making a new dish (you) and invites you in to observe the process.

It appears as if He has pulled out every spice in your cupboard and is now examining each one. You then watch Him carefully choose specific spices and dance a little jig as He sprinkles each one into the pot. He then mutters to himself,

"Let's see...I already put this and this in. What complements those flavors?"

And then all of a sudden, you jump back startled as He yells in excitement, "Oh! Oh! Oh! I've got it! I have to give her this! Oh, and I can't forget this one either. That's a PERFECT combination."

He then reaches for a spoon and carefully sips His gourmet meal; you watch as He squeezes His eyes closed, lifts His chin, and places His hand over His heart. Without a word spoken, you know He is in love with His creation.

As you lean into to view His beloved concoction, you notice the small collection of bottles He used to create you. You feel a warmth from knowing He was especially particular about the gifts He gave you.

And then a thought occurs to you.

"Wow. That's not very many spices."

As you begin to take in the entire kitchen scene, you spot on the counter the massive number of spices that God did not use to make you. And then you begin to worry.

Maybe you pick up a jar or two of those unused spices and read the labels.

Hospitality

Giving

Your worry then falls prey to panic, and you can't help but raise your voice and say just a bit too loud,

54

"But God! You forgot to put these in my dish! I must have hospitality! Every Christian woman is supposed to have hospitality!"

You quickly find your hands gently covered in His, and He is looking deeply into your eyes.

"Oh, my sweet girl. If I put all those spices in, that beautiful meal there would be completely inedible. Not to mention the smell. Terrible! You see, the spices I used *complement* one another.

Dear woman, I know you've been mad at yourself that hospitality doesn't come easily to you like your best friend, but my sweet daughter, I never meant you to have that spice. Just like I never meant for you to be a rock star mathematician or organizational guru. I didn't forget to give you those gifts. What I gave you was on purpose. I have a plan for your life and it doesn't need those gifts."

"But God," you say, "What am I supposed to do when a mom at church has a baby. Every woman knows you're SUPPOSED to take her a meal."

"Grab a Take and Bake Pizza from the store."

"Wait. What? I can do that? That counts?"

"It totally counts." God then picks up a bottle from the small collection on the counter. "And when you take that pizza to her and you see she is bedraggled and exhausted, you'll share this spice, 'Encouragement', giving her exactly what she needs in that moment, just like I planned."

Friend, you are made spicy not bland; those spices were chosen to give you a certain flavor. Each spice is a gift He gave you.

A good way to let go of the woman you think you should be and embrace the woman you really are is to find out who she is. Try to forget about the strengths you think you *should* have or wish you had and concentrate on the ones you do possess. The spices He intentionally put in you.

In 2016 my business coach stopped me in midsentence and spoke a truth that changed the trajectory of my life. She said, "Kathleen, I want to give you a bit of push back on something I hear you saying. You've mentioned several times your tendency to over think and overanalyze as if these are negative. But I want to challenge you to think of them as incredible assets. Your ability to think around an issue and find all the possible pitfalls is a gift. Do you realize companies pay big money for a brain like yours to help them create successful products?"

Mind blown.

What? My weaknesses are actually strengths? It was in that moment I began to give myself permission to embrace these parts of myself as lovely and valuable. Sure, unchecked they can cause issues, but my whole life I had believed there was *no* value to these abilities. I chalked it up to being a glass half empty negative person, and wishing desperately that God would someday fix me. And now, I see it was His plan all along. He made me this way to use me for good.

Maybe you have areas in your life you've counted as bad, negative, or faulty. My hope is you would challenge yourself to take a look at those things you've believed were liabilities and ask yourself if maybe they have real value.

In a Group or with a Friend

When Paul in the Bible talks about Spiritual Gifts, he calls believers to edify one another, to build each other up, and affirm one another's gifts.[5] Often it isn't until others close to us say, "You rock in this area, friend! That is so your gift," that we begin to accept our strengths. So, this is a perfect time to affirm each other.

If time allows, I would highly recommend allowing women to respond after each person shares in order to affirm and encourage one another that we all have strengths.

---

[5] I Thessalonians 5:11

Question 8:

What have you been told that you're good at that you've been known to discount? You may say "Oh, that's easy. Anyone can do that" or "that's not a big deal".

Have you included this strength to Question 7's answer?

Challenge: Ask someone who knows you well such as your spouse or best friend, "Which of my strengths do you see me downplay or devalue?"

Question 8: Kathleen's Thoughts

I stood back in amazement while I watched her create beauty in every corner of my home using my own things. Out of a disorganized storage box she pulled skeins of yarn, my grandmother's old teacups, and knitting needles to create the cutest décor in my office.

I asked her how she knew what to put where? She told me it was easy. Anyone can do it. I laughed. I laughed really hard.

My sister-in-law, Wendy can create beauty out of every day items. My friend Amy who is a writer, has an endless supply of stories running through her brain. They just come; she couldn't stop them even if she tried. Rachel, my lifelong friend naturally thinks of practical tangible ways she can support friends in desperate situations. Every woman I meet puts me in awe of what she just does without even thinking.

My gift of encouragement comes sidesaddle with the ability to spot people's gifts, and almost every single time I point to what I see, the woman across from me says, "Oh, that? That's easy. Anyone could do that." And then she'll proceed to tell me how simple it is. "All you have to do Kathleen, is _____." And that's when I laugh. Every time.

The gift she thinks is simple, is W.O.R.K. for me. I could do it, but it's not simple for me. It doesn't just ooze out of me without effort like it does for her.

Why do we tend to discount the easy? Why are the things that come naturally to us not considered our strengths? I wonder if it's because we assume in order for something to truly be a gift, it has be difficult. We have to sweat and toil while we work for it to count.

After having this same conversation on numerous occasions, I began to contemplate if there were a correlation between what comes naturally to us and our actual strengths and gifts. I think there is. If you want to know what you what you're good at, take a look at the compliments you dismiss.

In a Group or with a Friend

See In a Group or with a Friend from Question 7.

Question 9:

What do you wish you were better at?

Question 9: Kathleen's Thoughts

Yes, like our strengths in question 7, let's embrace our weaknesses too because that also was a part of your design, the way God made you. There were certain spices he didn't use because they weren't supposed to be part of your construction.

The idea here is to embrace all of you. Your struggles make you unique. And I think it's in the victories you experience in your weaknesses that God calls you to reach back, grab the hand of another woman struggling with the same challenge, and show her how she can begin to win. Your weakness then comes to the aid of another. And that, my friends is worthy of a celebration.

I've noticed in my Christian woman circles, many of us tend to focus much of our personal energy on *fixing* our weaknesses, while minimizing our strengths. If this describes you, I want to challenge you to consider that maybe God never intended for you to be good at those things. Maybe your job is to find a work-around, give the task away, or consult someone else who does have that strength.

I remember vividly the day God assured me the gift of hospitality was not a part of his plan for me. He let me know the reason that entertaining and coming up with meal ideas for other families in crisis was difficult. He never gave me those gifts.

And then the most brilliant thing happened; He encouraged me to reach out to other women with hospitality-gifted brains and ask for help. And wow! The jewels I've picked up from these precious ladies. These women have secrets that would blow your non-hospitality mind.

You know what else? These beautifully gifted friends were glad to help! Because I was asking them about something they find easy and fun. It was a delight for them to share with me.

Asking for help builds community. Chances are those you reach out to will feel affirmed in their own strengths. It's a win-win.

So, let's take the time to note our struggles, not to beat ourselves up, but to discover where we can build community and build up our other sisters.

In a Group or with a Friend

When a woman shares an area she wishes she is better at, there can be a tendency to feel discomfort and be tempted to jump in and say, "Don't feel that way!" or "Oh, but you *are* good at that." or "You are too hard on yourself." Those statements don't express empathy. Please see **Empathy and Traumatic Story Responses** (see Appendix) for examples of good empathy statements.

A better response would be, "Oh, wow. I didn't know you struggled with that. Boy, from the outside it looks like you are awesome at that." Or "Tell us some more about that because from my vantage point that has looked like a strength."

The difference in the empathic responses is that I am acknowledging she finds this area difficult; I am not trying to convince her to feel differently.

Question 10:

What is a negative thing you've told yourself that you know is untrue and/or unfair?

Question 10: Kathleen's Thoughts

There is something powerful about saying out loud the negative unfair/untrue things we tell ourselves. In 2016 I posted this question to the women in my Facebook group, Straight Up Real Mamas. The bravery and vulnerability women displayed by sharing what they tell themselves blew me away.

It was ugly and beautiful all at the same time. The ugly was how very mean we can be to ourselves; the beauty was the courage it took to write them out for everyone else to see. I saw women swoop in to affirm and encourage as another split herself open and lay her raw self before us. It was as if we all understood the unfair games we play with ourselves, and we needed to make sure each exposed woman was not alone.

In groups of women, it is not unusual for us to judge, criticize, and beat each other up with our words. But this day, with this question, that was not the case. And I wept.

Here is a bit of my journal entry that day:

"I read their negative thoughts and I cry. I cry because I've lived with those damning thoughts since I was a young girl, and I know they are flat out lies. I know if they would believe the truth about themselves and get out from under their own *should-ing*, they would fly and feel the wind in their face...the freedom of knowing they are beautifully and wonderfully made by God who is not disappointed or surprised they are flawed, but is rooting for them as they struggle."

I think we all saw we weren't alone. We all have the monsters in our heads that want to convince us we are not worthy.

I believe those monsters are the Enemy's handiwork. He wants you to keep you down and paralyzed by the lies.

Why this question? Two words: Brené Brown. She is a social science researcher who has studied connection, vulnerability, and shame since 2001. Out of her studies, she discovered shame cannot live when it is spoken; it can only survive when it has three things: Secrecy, Silence, and Judgment. Speaking our shame in the presence of safe friends can be truly powerful. Even if you never speak it aloud, simply writing it down could prove life altering.

In a Group or with a Friend

There may be a strong desire by many women to tell her friend to not feel that way. But please remember the best way to respond to a shame story is empathy. Please refer to **Empathy and Traumatic Story Responses** (see Appendix) before your group begins to share their answers to this question. The plan here is not to fix one another but to sit in each other's pain and connect.

Question 11:

Is asking for help difficult for you? What do you think contributes to this?

Question 11: Kathleen's Thoughts

There was a season in my life (bed rest for 12 weeks of my second pregnancy) when I was forced to ask for help. I could feel this inner conflict rumbling, screaming, "This is wrong! *I* help others; they're not supposed to help me."

I then began to get curious as to why it was difficult for me to accept help and better yet, why I struggled to ask for it. What was I telling myself that made asking for help feel awkward and borderline sinful? Yes, it felt sinful.

The answers went deep.

I had conditioned myself to think asking for help was selfish. I also saw it as a reflection of my own weaknesses. By asking for help, I would be admitting I couldn't do it all, and that was the ultimate evidence to the world I was failing.

It feels strange to write those words today because I can see how faulty that thinking was. If God created us to live in community with one another so that we lean on each other in our times of need, clearly he *designed* us all to have struggles and weaknesses. It was a part of the plan. We weren't meant to do it all ourselves.

I also did not consider what a blessing it was to the person who would get to step in and provide a helping hand. I thought it would be a burden for a friend to come run my laundry or bring my family a meal. As it turned out, my friends were excited to love on me in practical ways.

NOTE: I believe the power behind this question is the answers other women give. If you are not participating in an Embrace You Group (EYG), I want to challenge you to open a dialogue with other safe women in your life and ask them this question.

In a Group or with a Friend

Especially amongst Christian women, there seems to be an unwritten rule that since our job is about nurturing and assisting others, there is no room for the *selfishness* of asking for assistance for yourself. And yet we would never tell another woman to not ask for help. There seems to be a double standard here. It's okay for you to ask, but not for me. I'd love to hear what you discover.

Question 12:

Pick an age when you were a child. Now have that little girl (you) describe herself. Describe her physical looks, her character (what she was like as a person), her loves, her dislikes, and who she wanted to be when she grew up...

Start with "My name is _____ and I am _____ years old."

Question 12: Kathleen's Thoughts

I call this exercise the Out of the Womb Girl. This is about exploring who you were before the world got a hold of you and told you who you were and who you weren't. As you are digging in to discover and embrace you, there might be some real nuggets found here by looking back. There may be some keys to the real you hidden in that little carefree girl. You might even discover some loves you've forgotten about that you may want to revisit.

I want to reassure you that it's okay if you do not currently have access to your early childhood memories. After speaking at a women's retreat, a brave woman approached me and told me she was 3 years old when her sister passed away. Her only memories at that time included being sad and lonely. I suggested, if she were interested in learning more about her young self, she might ask the surviving adults for their observations. This could be a living relative who would have observed her before and after her tragic loss.

In our Embrace You Test Groups, many of the women had trauma as a part of their childhood story. Most opted to explore an age or time when she remembered being happy. So, please use this exercise however you want. If you want to explore the cheerful, happy memories, please do. If you came from a difficult home situation where there weren't many happy memories, feel free to explore those as well. There are no rules here. This process is about looking back at the raw material, seeing who you were back then, and appreciating that innocent little girl.

WARNING: If trauma was experienced in your little girl's life, this may not be a task you're ready to tackle. I give you full permission to skip this question. If you decide you want to give it a shot, please pay close attention to how your body, brain, and emotions react. If you feel shaky, anxious, breathing is difficult, or suddenly you feel quite angry at the dog for daring to want to be let outside, you may be getting triggered. At that point, I would encourage you to stop and do some self-care. See **Self-Care** in the appendix for ideas of how to do that.

I define trauma as any of the following events: divorce, abandonment, addiction, abuse, or death.

In a Group or with a Friend

Due to the fact this could be a triggering exercise to a woman's past trauma, I highly recommend the group read out loud **Empathy and Traumatic Story Responses** (see Appendix) prior to any sharing. In order to maintain a culture of vulnerability and safety, it is imperative your group responds with empathy. Without it, your group will die a sudden death and quite possibly cause more injury and damage to the affected woman. Please take good care of one another.

Question 13:

Write a letter to the little girl you've described in Question 12. Tell her what to be on the lookout for. If she needs to know something was not her fault, a divorce for instance, tell her. Tell her what you think of her and what parts of her you wish she'd keep.

Write what you need to write. For some, it may feel good to encourage her, or give her advice. Others may need to forgive her. It's important that this letter is whatever you need it to be now.

Question 13: Kathleen's Thoughts

Sometimes we blame ourselves for things we had no power to control. This question is meant to help you extend grace to your younger self. I've found that stepping back and seeing myself as a little person has sometimes helped make it easier to identify false truths and then forgive myself.

There have been times I've looked back to things I've done that I'm ashamed of and I think, "For crying out loud, you were 8 years old. What did you know back then? This doesn't define me. This mistake does not symbolize my character."

For me it was looking at little Kathleen and seeing how she loved being alone, playing with just one friend at a time when more than one created discomfort, and being in larger groups caused a feeling of deep uneasiness. It was also remembering I had been raised by an extrovert mom, who was struggling with her own identity at the time and was sure something was wrong with her little girl. Like any good mom who believes something is amiss, she tried to fix it. She worked to pull me "out of my shell" by forcing me to answer questions in front of large groups of people. Unfortunately, the message I received was, "There's something wrong with you."

Now I can look back and understand my mom's efforts, as well as tell little Kathleen that God made her to be reflective and pensive on purpose. Her love of close authentic friendships was placed in that little girl for a reason. In the future she would engage with women one-on-one and create a safe place for them to be honest about their real self. And finally, I can remind her it was through her need for quiet that allowed her to hear God speak into her life.

Please understand there have also been plenty of times when it's been crazy hard to forgive my little person. This is by no means a miracle-forgive-yourself exercise, but I believe it could give you a window into who you are and how you came to be the way you are today.

WARNING: If trauma was experienced in your little girl's life, please pay close attention to how your body, brain, and emotions react if you decide to do this exercise. If you feel shaky, anxious, breathing is difficult, or suddenly you feel quite angry at the dog for daring to want to be let outside, you may be getting triggered. At that point, I would encourage you stop and do some self-care. See **Self-Care** in the appendix for ideas of how to do that. Only come back to this exercise if you want.

I define trauma as any of the following events: divorce, abandonment, addiction, abuse, or death.

In a Group or with a Friend

Like in Question 12, due to the fact this could be a triggering question to a woman's past trauma, I highly recommend the group read out **Empathy and Trauma Story Responses** (see **Appendix**) prior to sharing each other's letters. In order to maintain a culture of vulnerability and safety, it is imperative your group responds with empathy. Without empathy, your group will die a sudden death and quite possibly cause more injury/damage to the effected woman. Please take good care of one another.

Question 14:

Complete this sentence, "I feel most alive when _____."

Question 14: Kathleen's Thoughts

Our culture today celebrates productivity and all kinds of busy. And for many women the clear message also seems to be you must take care of everyone (children, employees, aging parents, partner) and everything (domestic chores, children's school and activity schedules) before even considering yourself. Girl, let me remind you, God made you a human being with needs and desires on purpose. He created you to need to rest and refill your energy, love, and creative tanks. If you find yourself depleted and down, it may be time to review what makes you feel alive. And then go do that.

In a Group or with a Friend:

This could be a fun exercise in learning more about one another. Remember this also has the potential of creating a vulnerable space for women. It's important that we celebrate what makes each of us feel alive. It's a part of what makes us who we are.

If a group member struggles to come up with a list, it's okay to remind one another that we may be so used to taking care of the needs of everyone else, we are out of the habit of checking in with ourselves.

WARNING: There could be a temptation for you to compare yourself to other group members and then wonder if there is something "wrong" with you. For instance, a woman might have a more seemingly altruistic (self-sacrificing) aspect on her list like, "Serving a meal to the homeless." I want to encourage you not to beat yourself up. This is not a graded exercise. This is about embracing you, not what *should* make you feel alive. Also be cautious of our potential to think another woman's list is petty or selfish when it is unlike our own.

Question 15:

Have you had someone in your life who has loved you for who you really are? If so, what did they do to show you they accepted the real you?

What if there is no one who has ever accepted the real you?
Please read Kathleen's Thoughts.

Question 15: Kathleen's Thoughts

This question is meant to remind you there are people in this world who have loved you as is. My hope is that you would steep in that memory's feeling and then store it in an easily accessible place in your heart. Then later when fear shows up and tries to convince you that revealing the real you is a mistake, you could grab that memory and remind yourself you are worthy.

What if there is no one who has ever accepted the real you?

Maybe you've never felt you could let the real you out because it wasn't safe. First I want to say, "Good job taking care of you." Way to gauge the environment and protect yourself from folks who are not trustworthy. Second, I want you know that I think you are worthy. And I am confident that God knew what he was doing when he formed you in your mother's womb; His plan was to make the beautiful creature you are today. And finally, my hope is that as you uncover your most authentic self, you will begin to take some risks in finding your own Heart Holders (see **Identifying Your Heart Holders** in the Appendix). The process will feel a bit like an experiment, but the trick is, you are looking for someone who gets you, not someone you have to convince to get you.

For now, I would encourage you to explore what it would've been like to have someone accept the real you. What would they have said? What would they have done?

In a Group or with a Friend

Because there may be a woman in your group who is unable to answer this question because she feels there has never been anyone who has truly accepted her, it may be wise to read Kathleen's Thoughts before opening up for sharing. If the group feels it would be good to go over **Identifying Your Heart Holders**, this could be a great discussion after sharing is done. I find most women are wishing they had more Heart Holders in their life, but don't know how to find them.

Question 16:

Do you have any *real* friends? What makes them real?

Note: If you don't have any, what would make someone a *real* friend to you?

Question 16: Kathleen's Thoughts

I know we've already touched on what makes a Heart Holder, but I'd love for you to dig a bit deeper into this question. Get down to the nitty gritty details. It's there where you may discover a list of rules you use to measure a friend; yes, a list of what you value in a friendship. And this, my friend, is a part of who you are.

If you have found yourself in multiple bad friendships where you have not felt seen, heard, or valued, this list could aid you in the future when you meet new potential real friends. Before giving your heart away, use this list to help you decide if this woman meets your qualifications. Don't simply hand that beautiful heart to anyone.

The flip side of having a list of rules is you could miss out on some jewels. My recommendation: Hold your rules loosely.

One of the rules I discovered rolling around in my Real Friends Qualifications was a *real* friend cannot be easily offended. If I need to cancel a coffee date because my introvert nature is calling me to some alone time with my pajamas and Netflix, I don't want to worry that our friendship is now on shaky ground because I had to bail to take care of me. I need a friend who says, "Girl, I get it. You take care of you. Let's reschedule when Extrovert Girl comes out. I love you."

But then I had to decide, what to do if a *real* friend (someone I feel seen, heard, and valued with) *did* get her feelings hurt. Do I now write her off? Would I cross her off my Real Friend List? That seemed a little too extreme. But I guess that's what strict rules can do.

It became apparent that my Real Friends Qualifications needed revamping.

Which brings me to another list that also needed help. Before I met my husband I compiled the My Future Husband Must Have These list. Prepare yourself. You're going to laugh. Besides loving Jesus, earning an income, and having a solid plan for his future, he needed to have a pierced ear and play the guitar. I know. I'll wait for you to find your composure.

We can giggle at this young woman's list because those last couple seem insignificant to what would qualify a man as a good husband. Who cares about an ear piercing if he loves you and treats you well? By the way, he did have a pierced ear, but there was and never has been any guitar playing.

You may find the same with your rules for *real* friends. Just be careful to not compromise on the ones that count the most.

In a Group or with a Friend

What's so cool about this exercise is everyone in your group will have some same and some different criteria for a *real* friend. It may be fun to hear what your own Heart Holders value in friendship. You may learn something new about her.

WARNING: Please be kind to yourself if you find you do not meet every point on your Heart Holder's list. This is not about you making yourself be something you are not. We cannot be everything to everyone, right? Remind yourself she thought enough of you to have you in her EYG.

Also, remember you don't have to share everything you wrote down. You get to decide what is spoken and what is not.

Question 17:

Describe a time when you were brave or allowed
yourself to be vulnerable and you received favorable
results. Now describe a time when the results were
undesirable.

For each ask yourself:

- What did I feel before I chose to act?
- What did I feel after?
- Did it make me want to be brave again?
- If I were able to do it again, would I do it differently?

Question 17: Kathleen's Thoughts

"Courage starts with showing up and letting ourselves be seen."
- Brené Brown

My guess is you were brave in some way today. Maybe you showed up to the pick-up line at school with a messy bun and no make-up, shared a vulnerable part of your personal story with a friend, said no when yes would have been more comfortable, chose to not laugh at that coarse joke, or opted for family time over a popular after school event.

Chances are you are brave every day. I think it's important to take note of those times and give them their due credit *even* if the outcome was not desirable. Because, sweet friend, you took a risk and lived. That's worth giving you a pat on the back. You chose courage over comfort.

Brave for me lately has been choosing to listen to what my body, mind, and heart are saying they need more than to the loud, sometimes obnoxious voices of expectation, should, and obligation.

In the not too distant past (like yesterday) it was typical for me to say yes to things I didn't have the energy or time to do because I didn't want to disappoint people. The results were an exhausted me who had no energy reserves for myself or loved ones. My family got a lot of fumes for many years because I couldn't say no.

In my forties, I began to notice that my body would tell me when it was time to start saying no. This tense, balled up sort of feeling would show up when I was asked to volunteer or attend another graduation party. I have some very strong introvert tendencies. I love to speak to large crowds of people or have a deep conversation with one or two people, but put me in a social setting where small talk is prominent, and I would rather gnaw off my own hand. No joke.

I also noticed there were similar thoughts running through my brain like "If you don't do it though, there won't be anyone else. You'll leave them high and dry," or "They'll think you are lazy or you don't care about them."

I was placing a higher importance on how people saw me

above my own values of committing to things that fit within my energy level, family's health, and my own passions.

I am learning how to tell those thoughts to take a hike.

When my friend said she wanted to get together for coffee at a local cafe, I was totally up for it. I was in need of some girl time and I looked forward to it all week. We scheduled a 2-hour window to visit and catch up on one another's lives.

When the day arrived my friend realized she just didn't have the time she thought she would have. She still had a free hour if I wanted to drive out to her office. And if so, she asked if I would pick her up a coffee on the way.

You know how sometimes you can go with the flow and other times a change in plans unnerves you? This was one of those unnerving times. Every people-pleasing bone in my body wanted to say "Okay, no big deal." But then there was this other tense balled up part of me that was screaming, "Ugh! I don't want to drive 20 minutes each way, stop and buy coffee all for only 1 hour. I don't have it in me."

At that moment I decided to choose courage. I honestly told my friend I wasn't up to the drive, but would love to chat on the phone for an hour. So the next hour I got my girl time while comfortably wrapped in a fuzzy blanket and sipping a cup of homemade joe.

What I learned is I need to pay more attention to the voice that's telling me what I really want. The people pleaser gets to have input, but its voice does not get to be the loudest. When I allow the people pleaser to dominate my decisions, I often find resentment right behind it. If I had chosen to drive to my friend's office, I know I would have resented it. In that moment of honesty, I was choosing to take care of me as well as loving my friend.

In a Group or with a Friend

Before sharing answers to this question, it would be good to remind everyone how we may find ourselves uncomfortable when a woman shares her undesired results. It will be tempting to tell her all the reasons she shouldn't be embarrassed or hurt. Instead we want to practice empathy and not attempt to fix the situation. Please refer the group to **Empathy and Traumatic Story Responses** (see Appendix).

EMBRACE YOU

.

Question 18:

Complete these sentences:

"I want to be perceived as _____, _____, _____, & _____.
I don't want to be perceived as _____, _____, _____, & _____."[6]

Feel free to respond with as many words you'd like.

---

[6] Taken from <u>I Thought It Was Just Me</u> by Brené Brown

Question 18: Kathleen's Thoughts

I found this question in Brené Brown's book, _I Thought It Was Just Me But It Isn't – Making the Journey from "What Will People Think? To "I am Enough"_ in the chapter "Recognizing Shame." Dr. Brown uses these questions in workshops to help participants identify what triggers shame for them.

Throughout my life, there have been times when I have found myself completely paralyzed, unable to move toward a goal I would love to achieve because I am worried about what others will think of me. And don't even get me started when someone has given negative feedback on a project, writing piece or speaking engagement. Let's just say, I am a little uncomfortable with the thought I may unintentionally offend or hurt another person, and I will drive myself batty trying to do everything perfect to avoid that. For me it comes down to not wanting to be perceived as unintelligent or uncaring.

My friend Connie, who is a therapist, has told me on more than one occasion, "Honey, I just don't think you are that powerful." It makes me laugh every time because she's right.

I can't control what other people think of me.

And trust me, I've been working at it for 40 years. It can't be done.

Once I was the speaker for a large women's gathering and offended a schoolteacher in the audience. She did not appreciate that I bashed people who work for the public school system. Wait. I did what? I was mystified.

I then felt a wave of shame wash over me. I had used the illustration of a young girl's spirit getting crushed after she had started attending school. She struggled with reading and got the message she wasn't very smart. The purpose of the story was not to make a dig against the school system, but illustrate how even unintentional messages can be received and change how we see ourselves.

After working through the feeling I had just been called to the principal's office because I was in T R O U B L E, I took a step back and realized that what she perceived was not my intention. Some of my favorite people in the world are public school teachers. They know I love and respect what they do. They have also been incredibly valuable to me as I homeschooled my own two boys by sharing their teaching strategies as well as cheering me on. But because this woman didn't know me, she assumed that since I home schooled my own children, I was opposed to public schools and the work they do for our kids.

Even when we try every way possible to make sure people don't see us a certain way, invariably someone with their own perspective, life experience, and baggage will choose to perceive us in the way they choose. And we can't stop them.

So, the question for me has been, "If I can't stop them, will I continue to allow their opinion of me rule how I live?"

The answer I'm slowing arriving at is no. I am who I am. I am a whole mess of beauty, light, struggle, and dark. I will continue to grow and work to improve how I treat others and myself, but I want my values and passions to be my driving force.

I hope this question will help you recognize the perceptions you are trying to control, and maybe begin your journey of letting them go.

You are much more than other people's perspectives.

"It ain't what they call you; it's what you answer to." - W.C Fields

"And always remember that people's judgments about you are none of your business." - <u>Big Magic</u>, Elizabeth Gilbert

In a Group or with a Friend

It could be a wonderful thing to give the group a few minutes to respond after each woman shares and let her know how you each perceive her. But please be careful about saying no one sees her the way she doesn't want to be perceived; there is no way to know that.

Question 19:

Take a look at your list of the ways you don't want to be perceived from question 18 and ask yourself, "If people reduce me to this list, what important and wonderful things will they miss about me?" [7]

---

[7] Taken from I Thought It Was Just Me by Brené Brown

Question 19: Kathleen's Thoughts

The next time you feel misunderstood, grab this list and read it. Remind yourself who you really are.

If you struggle with this one, go back and review your answers to Questions 1 (what makes you happy), 7 (what are your strengths), and 8 (something you discount that others compliment).

In a Group or with a Friend

Please feel free to add to one another's lists.

Question 20:

Think about some times you felt you made a difference in someone's life and write about 2 or 3 of them. How did you feel in those situations?

Did the person notice?

Question 20: Kathleen's Thoughts

Is it me or are women in the 21st Century busier than ever before? We are not only racing around trying to be 100 levels above mediocre in our careers, parenting, housekeeping, and community involvement, but we also must care deeply about the environment, enjoy a rich and fulfilling time with the Lord on a daily basis, and be physically fit with a sexy body (but not too sexy).

We have an impossible standard to live by friends.

Have you noticed it is not okay to simply be okay at something? Who can measure up to this ridiculously high bar we have placed on each other and ourselves?

Um. No one.

Not even Wonder Woman. And that girl rocks!

Unfortunately, most of us are daily taking in images of our sisters kicking major booty in life that feeds this insatiable need to do it all. Am I right?

If you're feeling secure in your womanhood, a sure-fire way to knock you down a few (million) pegs is to just take a quick gander on Pinterest, Facebook, or Instagram where the success of our cohorts is staring us down, and highlighting our own shortcomings.

With these impossible standards that no woman could *ever* meet, we then can feel as if we aren't doing anything well.

Here's what I do know, friends: as tired as you are from keeping all the balls in the air, I can assure you, you *are* making a difference in someone's life. You are making an impact.

Please grab this moment to take stock of what you are doing well. The enemy would love to see you defeated, depressed, and overcome with feelings of uselessness. But that was never God's intention. He created you to win big in a few areas, but not all. And I definitely think he gets pretty excited when he sees us celebrating how he made us.

I would love for you to keep a running list of times when you've made a difference. And then in those moments when you feel you are not measuring up, you could come back and remind yourself, you are worth embracing.

In a Group or with a Friend

Some women may struggle to come up with an answer to this question. If that's the case, have everyone else in the group share first with the hope that she may get some ideas. You may even choose to help prime the pump for her before everyone shares by asking her to think of how she's made a difference in the following areas:

- At work?
- In a relationship with a friend, spouse, or child?
- With someone at church or a community group?

If you are looking for a bit more discussion, you could ask the group if they felt uncomfortable talking about themselves this way. For some, they've been taught that it's selfish to talk about the good they've done. I would agree, if that's all we ever did was self-congratulate to our friends, but my guess is most of us don't. Part of the work of embracing you is getting comfortable with who you are and how God designed you. And that means looking at the good and the bad.

KATHLEEN M. PETERS

APPENDIX

Self-Care

As you've probably discovered, embracing all the parts of you is not always easy. It can be hard work to dig around and look into your own light and dark places. That's why it's imperative to your own emotional health that you keep a watchful eye on how you're feeling and take measures to gently care for you.

What is self-care?

An enjoyable activity you do to take care of your own mental, physical, spiritual, or emotional health.

Why do I need it?

Self-care allows you to show up with your best self to work, relationships, and life. When you fill up your energy stores through self-care, you can then draw strength from them. If your emotional, physical, or mental stores are depleted, you will find yourself unable to operate at your full potential. And friend, the idea of Embrace You is for you to tap into your whole beautiful self, full potential and all.

Also, if you care for and tend to the needs of others, whether it is for family members or at work, your energy reserves most likely get regularly sucked out. Even when it's a pleasure to give to others, you will find yourself not being the best version of yourself if you don't keep replenishing those energy stores.

I know many of us have been taught that it is noble to sacrifice; that if you really love someone you will put his or her needs above your own. I see this played out especially with mothers. As much as I believe in sacrificing for those I love, I recognize there is a spectrum here. On one side there is neglecting my children and never attending to their needs, On the other is only focusing on the needs of my child and ignoring my needs completely. A more balanced approach would be taking 30 minutes a day to reset my mind, soul, and body. This makes me a better mom. It teaches my kids that I am a human with needs, loves, passions and not simply a person who takes care of them 24/7. It's important I model for them how to care for themselves when they are adults, but also that I am God's beautiful creation, not only a caregiver.

How do I know if I need self-care?

In my Facebook group, Straight Up Real Mamas, you can tell when a mama is in desperate need of self-care. You can hear it in her voice; she's exhausted and feels underappreciated and undervalued by her loved ones. She's been giving everything to everyone in her family.

Here's a list of indications that your energy stores are low:

1. I have a strong urge to run away.
2. I feel the need to numb or medicate. (alcohol, food, Netflix binge)
3. I get annoyed easily.
4. I often have strong negative emotions.
5. I feel overwhelmed or exhausted.
6. I have strong feelings of resentment ("No one appreciates all that I do." or "No one cares about me.")
7. I don't want to get out of bed.

8. I find it hard to get motivated.

What kinds of activities would be considered self-care?

Any activity that you enjoy really, but here are a few example possibilities:

A leisurely walk
Meditate
Take a bubble bath
Look at something pretty
Sit on the back porch
Color
Sleep – full 7-8 hours or a good nap
Exercise
Call a friend
Go for a drive
Read a book or magazine
Listen to music
Paint your nails
Take a hot shower
Journal
Go to a movie
Paint, Scrapbook, Knit
Hike in nature
Count the stars
Sing
Cancel something
Play an instrument
Try a new recipe
Bake cookies
Watch a movie
Say no to someone
Get a massage
Plan a weekend away
Pick a bouquet of flowers
Dance in the kitchen
Take photographs of a beautiful sunset
Pet the dog

Look at pictures of baby animals on Instagram

You don't have to spend hours every day in self-care either. But do make a point of planning to do something for at least 15-30 minutes every day that will recharge your batteries.

Identifying Heart Holders

	Graviate Towards	Shy Away From
How do I feel about myself when I am with her?	• Accepted • Approved • Appreciated • I have something to offer • Emotionally Safe • We're on Equal Standing	• Shame • Criticized • Judgement • Less or More Smarter than Her • Less of a Person
Is she vulnerable? (You're looking for mutuality)	• She struggles & shares with you • She seeks advice from you	• She seems to not struggle & has all the answers • She is the mentor in the relationship
How does she react when you tell her a shame story (something you did that was embarrassing/outrageous that showed you as imperfect)	• She listens and responds with compassion - "Oh man. That's hard. I hate that feeling." • She shares some of her own vulnerabilities not to one-up you - "I get it, I feel with you. I've been there." • "What do you need from me? How can I support you right now?" - asks for permission instead of sweeping into rescue	• She blames someone - "Where is that guy, I'm going to kick his butt!" • She's got to one-up you - "That's nothing, listen to what I did." • She scolds you. "How did you let this happen?" • She's going to make it better - "It wasn't that bad. You're exaggerating. Everyone loves you" • She feels shame for you. • She feels sympathy - "Oh, you poor thing" • She's disappointed in you. You've let her down

Empathy and Traumatic Story Responses

"When someone is drowning, they need you to throw them a flotation device, not a swimming lesson."

Most of us struggle to know what to say when a loved one goes through a traumatic experience. We know we want to provide them comfort, which by definition is to alleviate or fix their grief/pain. But the truth is there are no words to fix their pain. If we want to express our care and love to someone in the midst of the deep dark hole they are experiencing, our goal really would rather be to *empathize*.

Definition of Empathy[9]:

- To be able to see the world as others see it
- To be nonjudgmental
- To understand another person's feelings
- To communicate your **understanding** of that person's feelings

Here are few guidelines to help express empathy:

1. **Listen.**
   Show them you care by making the situation about them, not you. Speak little. Listen more.

2. **Use your body to express emotion.**

   - Eye contact
   - Head nods
   - Eyebrow movement to show surprise, sadness, etc.
   - Squeeze their hand or hug, with permission

---

[9] Nursing Scholar Theresa Wiseman's definition of empathy
Wiseman, T. (1996) A concept analysis of empathy. *Journal of Personality,* 42, 569-585

3. Use empathic statements only if needed.

Empathic Statements
That sounds really hard.
I don't know what to say, but I'm so honored you trusted me with this.
It seems like that took a lot of courage to share.
I hate that you have to go through this.
I bet you are (emotion they've expressed)! That's tough stuff.
I'm so sorry that happened to you.
Your story really touched me.
I love/appreciate/admire/respect you for what you've gone through.
I really relate to you and certain parts of your story.
Oh, man. That is so hard. I've done that dance. I hate that feeling.
Oh, friend! I hear you.
It sounds like you are in a really hard place right now.

Avoid Giving Advice or Fixing (can feel like criticism)
Just let it go. You need to move on.
Just stop thinking about it.
You need to forgive.
Stop being a victim; you are a survivor.
Don't feel that way.
Here's what I would do...
You need to confront them.
You'll be okay.
How's your Quiet Time with God? Maybe you need to pray more.
You know the Bible says....

Avoid Talking About You (gives impression you don't care)
I could never go through what you did.

I know exactly how you feel.
You think that was bad, listen to what happened to me…
When this happened to me…
The same thing happened to my aunt…

Avoid Asking for Details (intrusive & feels like you don't believe them)
Why did you _____?
Why didn't you _____?
What did he do next?
What happened? Tell me all about it.

Avoid Making a Silver Lining (minimizes their pain)
At least _____
Time heals all wounds.
What doesn't kill you makes you stronger
Just think of all the good that has come from it.
It's not that bad.
She's no longer in pain.
God must have needed another angel.

Sexual Assault and Sexual Abuse

Statistics tell us 1 out 3 women in the U.S. have been sexually abused. Chances are if you are in an Embrace You Group with four women, at least one has this as a part of her story. Please take note of things you do not want to say to her. Stick to the list of empathic statements and handle her heart with the utmost care.

Do Not Say to a Sexual Abuse Survivor
It sounds like you need to forgive.
The perpetrator must have terrible regret.
What were you wearing?
Was he/she drunk? Were you?
Did he rape you?
That almost happened to me, but I was a pretty smart kid.
Did you flirt?
Why didn't you __(stop it, tell someone, etc...)____?

Now I'm Sad

You probably know that talking about yourself when you are loving someone who is in pain is to be avoided, but what happens if that person's pain affects you so much that you now are struck with your own sad feelings? What if their trauma now triggers an injurous event from your own life? Can you talk about what you're feeling now?

The answer is yes and no. It depends on who you want to share with.

Psychologist Susan Silk and her friend Barry Goldman developed a Ring Theory[10] to aid us in determining who we can cry, complain, scream, or discuss how someone else's trauma has deeply affected us.

They tell us to draw a small circle and write the name of the person of whom the traumatic event has happened. Let's say Katy has breast cancer, her name would go in this circle. Around Katy we would draw a larger circle and place the name of her husband who is next closest to the painful event. And then we would proceed to add circles and names of people next closest to the trauma. Immediate family members would be in more central circles than distant relatives.

If you need to tell someone how shocked or upset you are, express how unfair it is, or cry, complain or scream, you would

---

[10] New York Times; April 7, 2013;
http://articles.latimes.com/2013/apr/07/opinion/la-oe-0407-silk-ring-theory-20130407

do this with those who are in a larger circle than your own and never to the smaller circles. Only empathy (comfort) statements go into smaller circles. Unless you were in the same circle, you would not want to break down (dump) in front of Katy's husband because he's too close to the trauma.

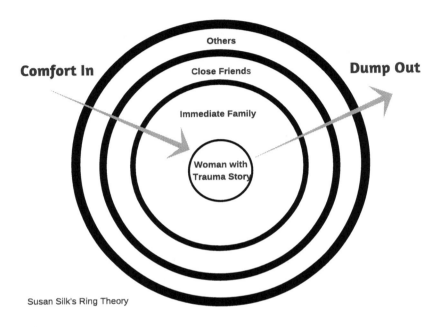

Susan Silk's Ring Theory

Want to Learn More About Empathy?

Check out my online Empathy course: https://kathleen-m-peters.teachable.com

Abuse Recovery Resources

Note: When perusing resources, it is possible you could find yourself triggered by what you run across. If you notice your heart racing, your breathing a little shallow, have panicky feelings, or anything else that doesn't feel quite right, you might want to take some space to breathe. Please be gentle with yourself.

Childhood Abuse/Child Abuse

Website

Child Abuse Resource Center
http://www.aacap.org/aacap/Families_and_Youth/Resource_Ce
nters/Child_Abuse_Resource_Center/Home.aspx
American Academy of Child & Adolescent Psychiatry

Articles

"Recovery from Childhood Trauma"
http://www.nacr.org/abusecenter/recovery-from-childhood-
trauma-2
by Juanita Ryan

"Recovery from Childhood Trauma: A Video Workshop with Juanita Ryan"
http://www.nacr.org/abusecenter/recovery-from-childhood-
abuse
by Juanita Ryan

"Residual Effects of Childhood Abuse in Female Adult Survivors"
https://www.goodtherapy.org/blog/residual-effects-of-
childhood-abuse/
by Joyce A. Thompson, MS, LMFT

Domestic Abuse

Websites

A Cry for Justice
https://cryingoutforjustice.com

Abuse Recovery Ministries and Services/ARMS
http://armsonline.org

Articles

"Choosing & Assessing a Counselor"
https://cryingoutforjustice.com/2015/03/30/choosing-assessing-a-counselor/
by Jeff Crippen and Barbara Roberts, A Cry for Justice

"What is Abuse? How Can I Identify an Abuser? How Can I Tell if I'm the Abuser?
https://cryingoutforjustice.com/how-can-i-identify-an-abuser/
A Cry for Justice

Books

The Verbally Abusive Relationship by Patricia Evans (Adams Media,, 2010);

Why Does He Do That? by Lundy Bancroft (Berkley Books, 2003);

Sexual Abuse

Website

RAINN
https://www.rainn.org

Article

"Healing Your Inner Child After Sexual Abuse"
http://www.pandys.org/articles/innerchild.html
Pandora's Project

Book

The Courage to Heal: A Guide for Women Survivors of Child Sexual Abuse by Ellen Bass & Laura Davis (William Morrow Paperbacks, 2008)

Spiritual Abuse

Online Course

"Introduction to Spiritual Abuse Recovery Essentials"
http://therapist-connie.teachable.com/p/religious-abuse-recovery-essentials-introduction
Connie Baker, MA, LPC

Websites/Blogs

Spiritual Abuse Recovery Resources
http://www.spiritualabuse.com

Spiritual Sounding Board
https://spiritualsoundingboard.com

The Wartburg Watch
http://thewartburgwatch.com

Book

The Subtle Power of Spiritual Abuse by David Johnson and Jeff VanVonderen
(Bethany House Publishers, 2005

General Resources

Articles

"Spiritual Abuse Is…"
http://southlakecounseling.org/spiritual-abuse-is/
by Shannon Thomas, LCSW-S, Southlake Christian Counseling

"10 Tips for Overcoming Perfectionism"
https://daringtolivefully.com/overcoming-perfectionism
Marelisa, Daring to Live Fully

"20 Diversion Tactics Highly Manipulative Narcissists, Sociopaths, and Psychopaths Use to Silence You"
http://thoughtcatalog.com/shahida-arabi/2016/06/20-diversion-tactics-highly-manipulative-narcissists-sociopaths-and-psychopaths-use-to-silence-you/
Shahida Arabi, Thought Catalog

"Are You Caring for Yourself in the Midst of Motherhood?"
https://faithfulmoms.org/caring-for-mom-in-motherhood/
Jessica Wells

"How Do I Break Up with a Destructive Friend?"/Shadow Selves
http://www.leslievernick.com/how-do-i-break-up-with-a-destructive-friend/
Leslie Vernick

"Strategies to Help Moms Avoid Compassion Fatigue"
http://www.huffingtonpost.com/entry/strategies-to-help-moms-avoid-compassion-fatigue_b_9042518.html
Shari Medini, Huffington Post

"Why 'Letting It Go' Is a Myth"
http://southlakecounseling.org/why-letting-it-go-is-a-myth/
Shannon Thomas, LCSW-S, Southlake Christian Counseling

Books

The Body Keeps the Score by Bessell van der Kolk (Penguin Books, 2015)

Boundaries: When to Say Yes, How to Say No to Take Control of Your Life by Henry Cloud (Zondervan, 2017)

Other Resources

"Listening to Shame"
https://www.ted.com/talks/brene_brown_listening_to_shame
Brené Brown, TED Talk

"The Power of Vulnerability"
https://www.ted.com/talks/brene_brown_on_vulnerability
Brené Brown, TED Talk

Godly Response to Abuse in the Christian Environment (G.R.A.C.E.)
http://www.netgrace.org/
The Mission of GRACE is to empower the Christian community to recognize, confront, and respond to the sin of child sexual abuse.

Say It Survivor
http://www.sayitsurvivor.com/
Say It, Survivor is non-profit organization committed to: Raising awareness and removing the stigma surrounding sexual abuse by telling our story shamelessly and encouraging other survivors to do the same.

S0-BEZ-716

Every Kid's
First Book of Robots
and Computers

David D. Thornburg

Published by **COMPUTE! Books**,
A Division of Small System Services, Inc.,
Greensboro, NC

A
Small System
Services, Inc.
Publication

To

harvey

01

Table Of Contents

COMPUTE! Books is a division of Small System Services, Inc.,
Publishers of **COMPUTE!** Magazine
Editorial Offices are located at:
625 Fulton Street, Greensboro, NC 27403 USA. (919) 275-9809.

Preface For Parents And Teachers

This book allows children to develop skills in computer programming and geometry through the use of a commonly available toy – the Big Trak robot vehicle. Programming is introduced as the communication tool through which the child conveys instructions to the machine. Once the machine's language limitations are understood, it can be made to follow any procedure which has been entered by the user. The mastery and control of a simple and inexpensive "computer" such as the Big Trak thus becomes the training experience that allows children to create their own programs on larger desk-top computer systems. There are many reasons for having children learn to program computers. The computer is one of the many tools which will be commonplace in our children's lifetime. To deny children computer literacy is as nonsensical as denying them the opportunity to learn to read.

It is always exciting to find a plaything that, when viewed in a different light, is also a valuable educational tool. Simple geometric blocks, for example, take on additional educational value when combined with a mirror to allow the exploration of geometric symmetry. While most toys have recognizable educational content, many parents and teachers familiar with programmable robot vehicles (such as the Big Trak) have yet to discover the value of these toys in teaching geometry and computer programming. In the several years this product has been on the market, a few colleagues and I have used it in numerous classrooms and workshops. We have used it to teach programming to children from first to sixth grade, and have found the experience to be rewarding for both the children and their teachers.

Vehicles such as the Big Trak belong to a class of robots known as "turtles." A turtle responds to incremental commands (for example, GO 10 units, or TURN 90 degrees). By issuing commands to move or turn by various amounts, the turtle can be instructed to trace out a path that defines any geometric shape. The process-based descriptions characteristic of turtle geometry are to be contrasted with the static descriptions of objects given by traditional coordinate geometry.

One of the turtle's major advocates in this country is Seymour Papert. He and his colleagues at the Massachusetts Institute of Technology have spent many years implementing and using turtle geometry in a computer language called LOGO. Much of Papert's philosophy regarding the use of computers by children was influenced by his association with the Swiss psychologist and educational philosopher Jean Piaget. In Papert's book, *Mindstorms: Children, Computers and Powerful Ideas* (Basic Books, 1980), the computer is described as an adaptive tool to which the child can "teach" various concepts. In the course of conveying procedures to the computer, the child learns the concepts as well.

Our use of turtle commands as the programming language mirrors the process-based descriptions commonly used by children. For example, a child is likely to describe a nearby location, such as a friend's house, by a procedure (Go two blocks, turn right, go another block, turn left, ...). Because turtle geometry has been incorporated as the graphics environment in several computer languages available for the popular desk-top personal computers, these programming ideas can continue to be used as the child learns to operate other computers.

The material in this book has been tested with children of many ages and skill levels. Our use of multiple levels of abstraction reinforces basic concepts and provides the bridge to other computer environments. As for the utility of such environments, all the illustrations for this book were prepared on an Atari 800 computer using turtle graphics in the language Atari PILOT. The resulting pictures were printed on an Epson MX-100 printer using the Screen Printer Interface from Macrotronics.

Additional books on similar topics include *Turtle Geometry: The Computer as a Medium for Exploring Mathematics,* by Harold Abelson and Andrea diSessa (MIT Press, 1981), and *Picture This! PILOT Turtle Geometry: An Introduction to Computer Graphics for Kids of all Ages,* by David Thornburg (Addison Wesley, 1982).

Many of the basic approaches in this book, including the development of a unique programming tool, Turtle Tiles, benefited from numerous discussions with Liza Loop. As one of the people who pioneered the use of programmable toys in the classroom, her firsthand experiences reinforced my own and strengthened my determination to complete this project.

I have also been encouraged to work in this area by many teachers and by many people in the computer community. While a list of any reasonable size would be incomplete, I wish to acknowledge Portia Issacson, Ted and Robert Kahn, and Seymour Papert as just a few of the people who helped to guide my work.

My greatest encouragement has come from the children who have been introduced to computers through early drafts of this book. It is their excitement, playfulness, and love of learning which, more than anything else, convinced me of the value of the turtle in education.

CHAPTER ONE

Let's Meet A Robot!

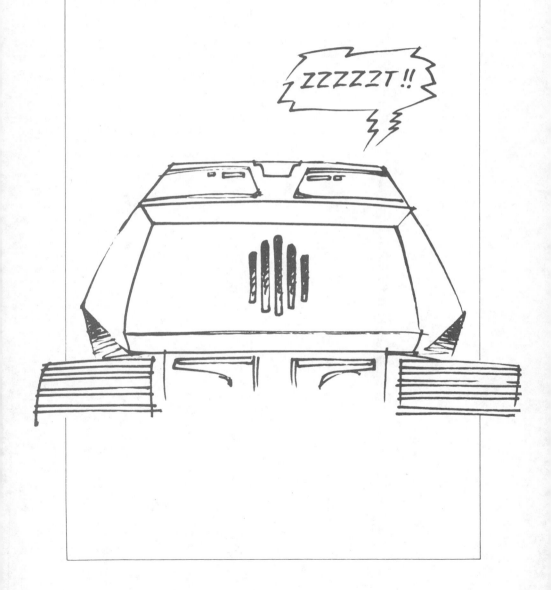

Suppose you had a machine that could follow your instructions. How would you ask it to do something?

Maybe we need to decide just what kinds of things it is that this machine can do. If it knew about music, maybe it could play us a song. Or if it knew about cooking, maybe it could give us a snack. There are lots of things we could ask machines to do for us. That is why people build machines in the first place.

This book is about some special machines called *robots.* Do you know what a robot is? A robot is a special device that can move itself around in response to our instructions.

There are lots of reasons you might be interested in robots and computers. If you think robots are only found in the movies, you are in for a surprise. To start with, there are several interesting toys such as the Milton Bradley Big Trak that are real robots. By learning how to give instructions to machines like the Big Trak, you will be learning some things that will make it easier for you to use your own computer. Who knows — someday you might even be working in an area where your interest in robots and computers will be valuable!

Imagine what it would be like to have a robot around the house. Just think — you could say "Make the bed," and the robot could make your bed up in the morning. You could say "Take out the garbage," and the robot would do it without even saying "YUCHHH!"

Project 1. Make a list of at least ten chores that could be done by a robot.

Next to each chore, write the command you would want to give to the robot in order to make it do the chore for you.

If you take a good look at your list, you might notice that each chore probably seems pretty simple for *you* to do. The robot, of course, can't make the bed or take out the garbage without being told how. Let's look at the task of taking out the garbage. How do *you* do it? First you have to pick up the wastebasket, then you have to go out the door, turn right at the patio, go to the garbage can, lift the lid, throw in the garbage, replace the lid, and retrace your path back into the house.

Whew!

If we are going to have a robot do this for us, we need to find out exactly how to get each of these steps into the robot's set of instructions.

Maybe we should start by looking at the basic instructions a robot needs to follow in order to do *anything* useful. Without thinking *too* hard you can probably come up with two important instructions right away.

For starters we will look at the instructions FORWARD and TURN. Let's pretend that our robot is a mechanical turtle that can crawl along the floor as it follows our commands. We will show the turtle as a triangular arrowhead because this way it is easy to see in which direction it is pointing.

If we tell the turtle to go FORWARD it is

almost ready to wander off in whatever direction it is headed, but it needs one more piece of information. What else do we need to tell the turtle? We need to let the turtle know how *far* to go forward. This amount will be a number. If we say FORWARD 5 the turtle will not travel as far as if we say FORWARD 25.

But what do 5 and 25 mean? Do we want the turtle to go 5 centimeters, 5 miles, 5 zillionths of a yard? Five what?

Well, since it is our robot, I guess we can make the number represent anything we want — a "turtle unit." Let's define 1 turtle unit to be the length of the turtle itself. This means that if we say FORWARD 1, the turtle will advance forward by one turtle unit.

FORWARD 1

If we say FORWARD 1 again, the turtle will take another step.

FORWARD 1
FORWARD 1

Now let's get brave. We can say FORWARD 78.

FORWARD 78

Whoops! Hey, turtle — come back here!

Oh boy — that dumb turtle just wandered out of sight and we don't even know how to get it back.

We need another command so that we can have the turtle change direction. We need the command TURN. After all, it would be a pretty boring turtle if all it could do is wander off in one direction without being able to turn.

Clearly, if we want the turtle to TURN, it can't do anything until we tell it how much. The most common numbers for measuring turns are in units called *degrees.* If you turn around in a complete circle, you will have turned exactly 360 degrees.

If we say TURN 90, the turtle will turn to the right like this:

TURN 90

If we say TURN 90 again, the turtle will now be pointing backwards:

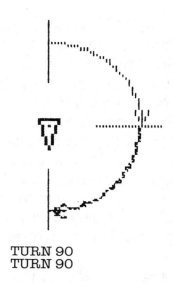

TURN 90
TURN 90

If we give this command twice more (TURN 90, TURN 90), we get back exactly where we started.

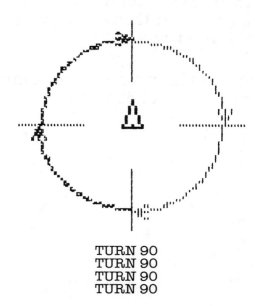

TURN 90
TURN 90
TURN 90
TURN 90

We have turned the turtle by
90 + 90 + 90 + 90 degrees, or 360 degrees
overall.

Just as FORWARD always moves the turtle
(starting from wherever it is at the time) TURN
always turns the turtle from the position it
was pointing at the start of the turn.

Now that we have both FORWARD and
TURN, we can use combinations of these to
make the turtle go anywhere we want. We go
as far as we want in one direction, turn the
turtle by some amount, and then have it go
some distance in the new direction. By
repeating this sequence of commands, we can
make the turtle follow almost any path.

Project 2. You should spend some time
thinking about the commands FORWARD
and TURN. Can you describe how to get
from your home to the store or school by
using these two commands? Is there
any path you can think of that *can't* be
described this way?

Next we will show how these commands
are used with a real robot turtle.

CHAPTER TWO

Introducing Some Turtles

There are lots of machines in the world that can accept commands of the type we have just described. Before going much farther, it is important that *you* get your hands on a robot turtle so that you can experiment with making it move in various ways instead of just reading how to do it.

We will concentrate on two turtles — the Big Trak robot car made by Milton Bradley, and Turtle Tiles — a set of cardboard turtle paths that allow you to try turtle instructions out any time or anywhere. A set of Turtle Tiles is included with this book.

We want this book to be useful to you whether you have a Big Trak or not. When we are covering general turtle information, we will use the triangular turtle symbol at the start of the section.

When we are covering Big Trak information, we will use this Big Trak symbol.

And, when we are covering Turtle Tile information, we will use the Turtle Tile symbol.

As each new idea is tried out, we will illustrate the concept three times — once for each of our turtles. This way you don't have to worry about missing anything if you don't happen to have a Big Trak handy, or if you left your Turtle Tiles at a friend's house.

Using The Big Trak ...

If you don't already have one, you can buy a Big Trak from most toy stores for under $50. This robot car is a terrific turtle for you to use along with this book. The Big Trak also has some accessories, such as a dump cart. We will only use the Big Trak by itself, so if you have any accessories for this machine, you might leave them aside for a while.

The Big Trak has a keyboard on its top that looks something like this:

	▲		CLR
◄	HOLD	►	FIRE
	▼		CLS
7	8	9	RPT
4	5	6	TEST
1	2	3	CK
IN	0	OUT	GO

To make this turtle move around in a specific path, you first have to push the buttons in the correct sequence to store your instructions in the turtle's memory bank.

Let's look at how we can make the Big Trak do some of the things we have described. Let's make it go FORWARD and TURN.

The very first thing you have to do is be sure that you have fresh batteries in your Big Trak. Check the instruction book that came with your unit to see how this is done. Next, turn on the Big Trak by sliding the grey switch located just above the keyboard.

> **A special note.** Whenever the Big Trak is turned on (but not doing anything) it will "beep" at you every so often to remind you that it is ready for action. If you are not going to use your Big Trak for a while, be sure and turn it off to save the batteries.

Press the key marked CLR. The letters CLR stand for the instruction *clear.* This key will clear the Big Trak's memory bank of any instructions it has stored. Next, look for the key that looks like an arrow pointing up. This key is shown in the figure.

This key corresponds to the FORWARD command. When you press this key (go ahead and do it!) you will hear a beep. If you don't hear the beep, check to be sure the power is turned on and that the batteries are fresh. This beep sound lets you know that the Big Trak has received your instruction. If you press this button again, you won't hear the beep because the unit already knows *what* it is supposed to do. It just doesn't know *how much* to do it.

Look at the keyboard again to find the numerals 0 through 9.

7	8	9
4	5	6
1	2	3
	0	

Press the numeral 1. As soon as you do this you will hear another beep to let you know that this number has been accepted into the memory bank. By pressing these two keys, you have told the Big Trak to go FORWARD 1.

Next, press the key marked CK. The letters CK stand for the instruction *check*. After making a few beeps and whistles, your Big Trak will move forward by one turtle unit. The CK commmand lets you check instructions step-by-step as they are entered. Whenever CK is pressed, the Big Trak will do whatever you told it to with the most recently entered command.

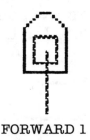

FORWARD 1

If you enter FORWARD 1 again, and press the CK key, your turtle will move one more unit along the floor.

FORWARD 1
FORWARD 1

Next, let's see the Big Trak move greater distances. Enter FORWARD 17 and press CK. Wow! There it goes — your Big Trak is heading off for a long trip, seventeen units long. Fortunately, this turtle moves slowly enough for you to chase after it.

Why don't you do an experiment to see

how far the Big Trak can go with a single
FORWARD command?

Now that we can make the Big Trak go
forward, we need to know how to make it turn.
If you look at the keyboard you will see a key
that looks like an arrow pointing to the right.
This key is highlighted in the figure below:

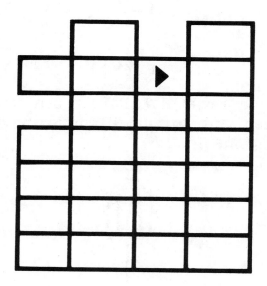

If you push this key, you will hear a beep
that tells you that the Big Trak has accepted
the command to TURN to the right. As with
the FORWARD key, nothing will happen if you
press this key again.

We must now let the Big Trak know how
much we want it to turn. Let's enter 90 and see
what happens. If this number were a measure
of the turning angle in degrees, then TURN 90
would turn the Big Trak until it was facing to
the right. After entering 90, press the CK key
to see what happens.

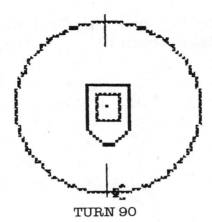

TURN 90

Wow! Instead of turning 90 degrees to the right, the Big Trak turned around one and a half times! Apparently this means that Big Trak's turning angle is *not* measured in degrees.

Let's do an experiment to see if we can figure this out. Set the Big Trak pointing straight out in front of you. Since TURN 90 turned the turtle one and a half times, what number should we have entered to make it turn in one complete circle? Let's try turning 60 units and see how that works. Enter TURN 60 and press CK.

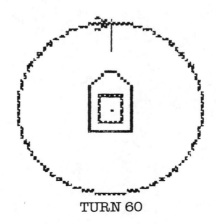

TURN 60

Depending on your Big Trak and the kind of floor surface you are running it on, this command should turn your turtle in one complete circle. You may have to experiment with different turning angles to find one that turns your Big Trak in an exact circle. Make note of this value. We will always assume that there are 60 Big Trak turning units in a circle, even though you might get a slightly different number.

Using The Turtle Tiles ...

In case you haven't already done so, go to the back of this book and carefully remove the cardboard Turtle Tiles. Notice that each Turtle Tile is in the shape of an octagon and has a front and a back that look like this:

FRONT   BACK

Start by setting one Turtle Tile on the table in front of you like this:

This tile will always be left here as a marker to show where you started. To follow the command FORWARD 1, you just connect a second tile to the first so that the bottom edge of the new tile connects to the head of the first tile.

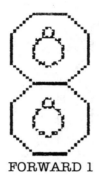

FORWARD 1

Next we will issue the command FORWARD 1 again. To follow this command, you should flip the front tile over to the turtle path side and then place a third tile at the end of this path. Be sure that the turtle's head is pointing forward — we haven't turned yet!

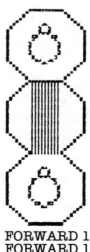

FORWARD 1
FORWARD 1

This path is two turtle units long. The lines in the figure below show how the length of the turtle path is measured from the center of each tile.

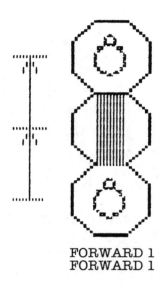

FORWARD 1
FORWARD 1

Now that we know how to make our turtle go forward, we need to examine the TURN command. You may have noticed that each Turtle Tile has eight sides. Each tile is an *octagon*. As you turn a tile on the table you will find eight positions where its edges will line up with the original position. See if you can convince yourself that these are the only eight positions of this sort you can find.

Next place a single tile in front of you. If you give the command TURN 1, you turn the tile like this:

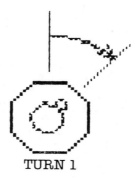

TURN 1

This corresponds to turning the tile by 1/8th of a circle. If you are used to measuring angles in degrees you might notice that this amount of turning is 45 degrees.

Next, let's start from our beginning position and give the command TURN 2. When you turn the tile two units, it will be pointing to the right. This means we have turned 90 degrees from our original position.

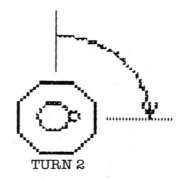

TURN 2

As you will see in the next chapter, even these limited turning angles can let us explore some interesting pathways for our robot turtle.

CHAPTER THREE

Moving In A Square
Our First Turtle Pathway

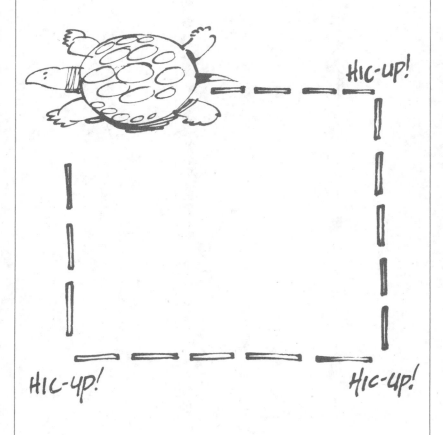

HIC-UP!

HIC-UP!

HIC-UP!

The commands FORWARD and TURN are very powerful because they can be combined in ways that let us describe any path we want the robot to take. In this chapter we will explore how to combine these commands to produce a complete set of instructions for making the robot turtle trace out a square path. To do this we will make what is called a *procedure*. A procedure is a set of instructions that the robot can follow to go in paths more complex than those made with a single FORWARD or TURN command.

To get started, take a pencil or pen and draw a square on a sheet of paper. How did you do it? Did you draw four connected lines one after the other like this?

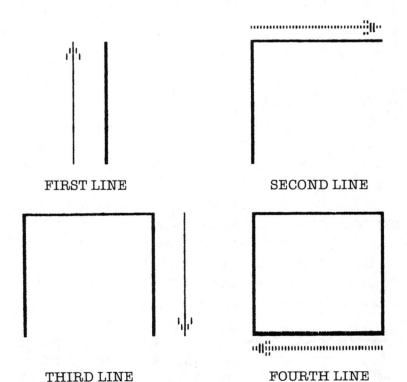

FIRST LINE

SECOND LINE

THIRD LINE

FOURTH LINE

That is a perfectly good way to draw a square. There are lots of other ways of drawing squares also. For example, we could have drawn the vertical sides first, and then drawn the horizontal sides.

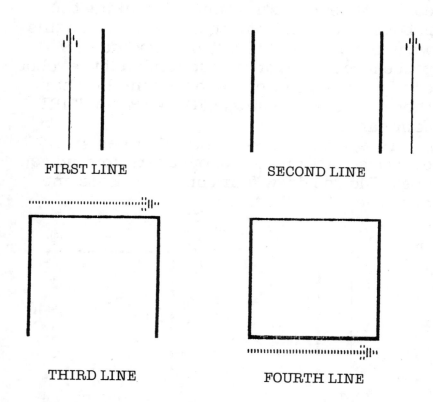

FIRST LINE   SECOND LINE

THIRD LINE   FOURTH LINE

While this is a perfectly good way for *you* to draw a square, it is not very useful for our turtle, simply because each new line does not start from the ending point of the previous line. Even though you end up with a square, you have not drawn a square path.

Project 3. How many ways can you draw a square? Lines that are drawn top to bottom are different from lines drawn bottom to top, so don't miss these ways when you count them up. Out of all the ways you have found to make a square, how many of these are useful paths for a robot to follow?

Once a path is finished, you often can't tell how it was made. From the turtle's point of view, the *path* is very important. It wouldn't be useful, for example, to have robot move through a solid wall just because it might be the shortest path between two points of interest.

SQUAREPATH For The Turtle ...

Using the commands FORWARD and TURN let's figure out how to move the turtle in a square. We can start by picking the length of our square's side. For the size turtle we use in this book, let's pick a length of 4. First we give the command FORWARD 4.

FORWARD 4

Next we have to turn the turtle to the right by 90 degrees with the command TURN 90.

TURN 90

Notice that the turtle didn't move forward when this command was given, it only turned. Now we can finish the square by using these commands some more:

FORWARD 4
TURN 90
FORWARD 4
TURN 90
FORWARD 4

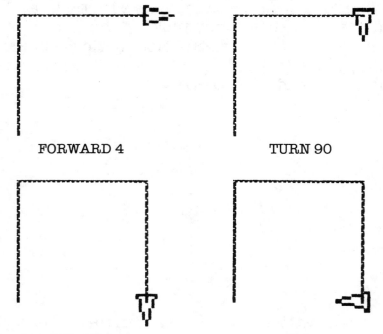

FORWARD 4　　　　　　　　　TURN 90

FORWARD 4　　　　　　　　　TURN 90

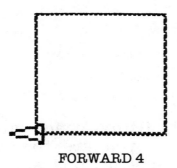

FORWARD 4

Now the turtle is back at the starting point
— or is it? Even though the square appears
finished, look at the turtle. Is the turtle back
where it started? Remember that, when we
started, the turtle was pointing straight up. It
is now pointing to the left. To complete our
square path we need one more TURN 90
command to get the turtle pointing straight
up again.

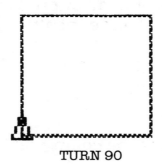

TURN 90

This completes the procedure
SQUAREPATH. The whole procedure is shown
below for reference.

```
SQUAREPATH
   FORWARD 4
   TURN 90
   FORWARD 4
   TURN 90
```

```
        FORWARD 4
        TURN 90
        FORWARD 4
        TURN 90
END
```

Project 4. Using pencil and paper, pretend that you are the robot and follow the instructions shown above. Instead of making the last 90 degree turn, keep pointing to the left. Now, follow the procedure again, starting from this new direction. Will your path be different from the original square? How many times will you have to repeat this process before you retrace the original square?

Now that we have worked out a procedure for having the turtle move in a square path, let's do an experiment. Suppose we start with the turtle in its "home" position.

Next we give the command TURN 45.

TURN 45

At this point, let's have the turtle use the procedure SQUAREPATH.

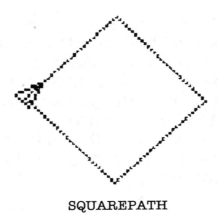

SQUAREPATH

As you see, the turtle now moves in a diamond-shaped path.

One of the most valuable features of procedures is that they can be used along with other commands and procedures to greatly increase the number of things the robot can do. Our procedure SQUAREPATH can be used to make the turtle follow a square path from any place the turtle happens to be when we issue the command. This means that we don't have to make different procedures for squares with different starting points or starting angles.

Each time we define a new procedure, we *extend* the number of commands the turtle can obey.

SQUAREPATH For The Big Trak...

Now it is time for us to enter the procedure SQUAREPATH in the Big Trak robot. First turn on the Big Trak and press the key marked CLR. You are now ready to enter the procedure on the keyboard. While you can use any path length you want (depending on the size floor you are using), we will use paths whose length are two units in our example.

First enter FORWARD 2 and press CK. As soon as this key is pressed, your Big Trak will move forward two steps.

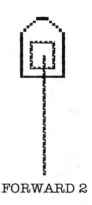

FORWARD 2

Next, enter TURN 15. (Remember that we want to turn 90 degrees to the right. If your Big Trak needs a different turning angle to do this, enter your number instead of 15.) When you press CK again, the Big Trak will turn to the right.

TURN 15

Now enter the rest of these commands, pressing CK after each command is entered.

    FORWARD 2
    TURN 15
    FORWARD 2
    TURN 15
    FORWARD 2

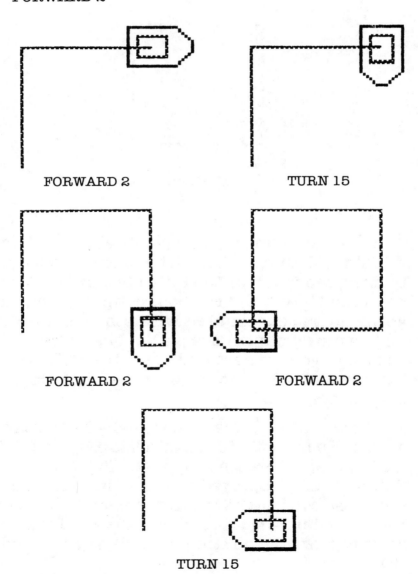

FORWARD 2

TURN 15

FORWARD 2

FORWARD 2

TURN 15

If everything went according to plan, your Big Trak robot is back home — except for one thing. We forgot to make the last turn! Enter TURN 15, press CK, and you should be right where you started.

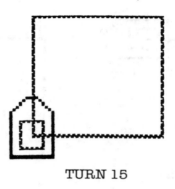

TURN 15

If you are almost (but not quite) back where you started, this means that you are either turning too much or too little at each TURN command. Don't worry about being perfect, but go ahead and experiment with other turning angles until your square path looks pretty square to you. Be sure and press the CLR key before entering a new set of SQUAREPATH commands!

Now that we have made the Big Trak go in a square path, let's do it again the easy way. Each time you pressed a key, the Big Trak automatically captured this information and put these commands into a procedure. To use the procedure that is stored in the Big Trak, set it in front of you and press the key marked GO.

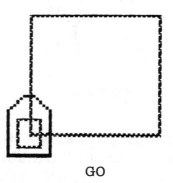

GO

The Big Trak will now trace out the complete square path each time you press a single key — the GO key.

This procedure will stay in the Big Trak until you do one of two things. If you press the CLR key or turn the Big Trak off, you will erase any stored procedure from the turtle's memory. For this reason, you should always keep a written record of any paths you create so that you can re-enter them as you need them.

Big Trak procedures can be up to 16 instructions long. If you try to enter longer procedures, the Big Trak just won't accept them. You will no longer hear the "beep" when you press keys on the keyboard.

Now that SQUAREPATH is safely stored in the turtle's memory, let's make the Big Trak travel in a diamond path. Set the Big Trak in front of you.

Next enter TURN 7 and press CK.

TURN 7

This turned the Big Trak by about 45 degrees to the right, but it also added one more instruction to our procedure. To erase this step from the procedure, press the key marked CLS *once*. The letters CLS stand for the instruction *clear step*. Each time CLS is pressed, it erases one step from the procedure stored in the Big Trak. The CLS key is handy for fixing mistakes without having to press CLR and start over.

Next press GO and see what happens.

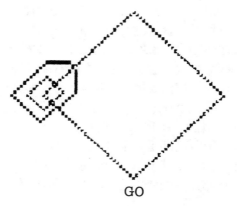

GO

Our Big Trak has just traced out a diamond shaped path.

The steps we used to create procedures in the Big Trak are easy to summarize.

1. Turn on the Big Trak and press CLR to clear the turtle's memory.

2. Enter each step and press CK to make sure it works properly.

3. Fix any bad steps by pressing CLS and entering the correct command. (Be sure to move the Big Trak to the end of the previous step before pressing CK again).

4. When you are done, press GO to see the Big Trak carry out your whole procedure!

SQUAREPATH For The Turtle Tiles ...

To illustrate SQUAREPATH with the Turtle Tiles, we first have to pick a path length. We will use two units in our illustration, but you have enough tiles to make a square at least six units long on each side.

Start out with one tile face up on the table in front of you and follow the command FORWARD 2.

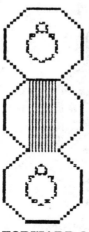

FORWARD 2

Next, to turn 90 degrees to the right, use the command TURN 2. To follow this command, take the end tile and turn it to the right like this.

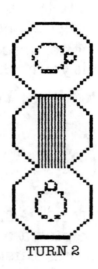

TURN 2

Now follow the rest of the commands.

FORWARD 2
TURN 2
FORWARD 2
TURN 2
FORWARD 2
TURN 2
FORWARD 2

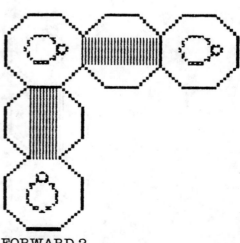

FORWARD 2

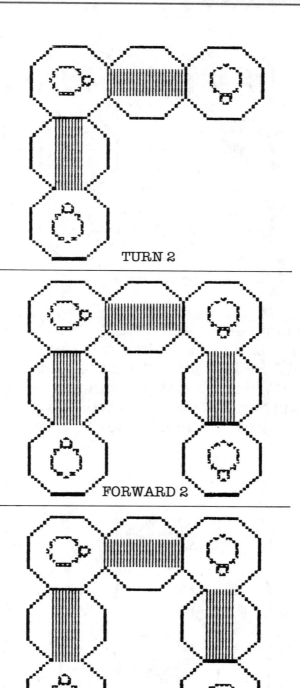

TURN 2

FORWARD 2

TURN 2

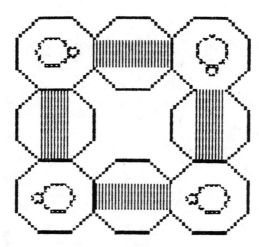

FORWARD 2

The last tile should be laid over the very first tile in the path. As in our other examples of SQUAREPATH, notice that the turtle is in the correct place, but is pointing in a different direction than the one from which it started out. To fix this we just add the command TURN 2.

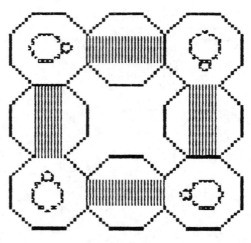

TURN 2

This finishes our square path!

One of the really neat things about Turtle Tiles is that they let you see the path the turtle took as it moved around. This means that you can create any path you want with the Turtle Tiles, and can then "read" the procedure for making this path by just looking at the tiles.

Let's try this out to see how it works. The figure below shows a complete turtle path, with the starting position marked.

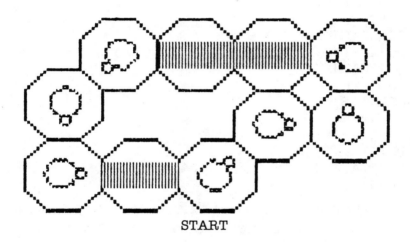

START

What are the commands used in the procedure that generated this path?

First, notice that the starting position is turned 45 degrees from our home position. This means that the first command must be TURN 1. Next, the turtle went FORWARD 1 and TURNed 1 again. After this, the turtle went FORWARD 1 and then it turned to the left instead of to the right.

Hmmm — how do we turn to the left? There are several ways to do this. One way is to use negative numbers to turn to the left — for example, TURN -2. Another way is to realize that since TURN 8 turns us in one complete circle, if we instead turned six units (8-2) we would be pointing to the left.

See if you can convince yourself that the complete procedure for the path shown above is this one:

```
TURN 1
FORWARD 1
TURN 1
FORWARD 1
TURN -2
FORWARD 1
TURN -2
FORWARD 3
TURN -1
FORWARD 1
TURN -1
FORWARD 1
TURN -2
FORWARD 2
TURN -1
```

As you can see from this example, you now have a new tool to help you write procedures for your robot. First, use your Turtle Tiles to map out the complete path you want to follow. Then write down the commands the turtle has to use at each step of the path.

In the next chapter we will learn something that *all* closed turtle paths have in common.

CHAPTER FOUR

The
Total Turtle Trip

Procedures like SQUAREPATH are special turtle pathways because they always end up where they started out. When the turtle goes on a trip of this sort it is called a *closed path*. If you think about it, closed paths are probably a very common part of your life. In the morning you leave for school and then you return home again in the afternoon. You make many trips like this — going to the store, visiting a friend, even going on a vacation trip. All these trips start and stop at the same place.

You already know that you can go to school by one path and come back by another. No matter which path you take, you still end up back home. In this chapter we are going to find out what makes closed paths so special.

Some Trips For The Turtle ...

Using the commands FORWARD and TURN, let's examine several closed paths and see what they have in common. The first path we will make is a triangle. Let's pick three units for the length of each side. A procedure to draw a triangle looks like this:

```
FORWARD 3
TURN 120
FORWARD 3
TURN 120
FORWARD 3
TURN 120
```

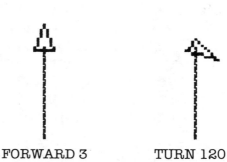

FORWARD 3   TURN 120

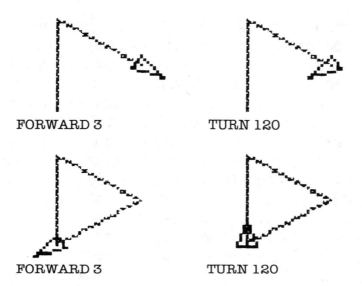

FORWARD 3   TURN 120

FORWARD 3   TURN 120

As you can see, this gives us a triangle with three equal sides. Now that we have the turtle back at its home, let's do two things. Let's figure out how far the turtle moved and how much it turned on its trip. The turtle went forward three units on each side of the triangle, making the trip nine units long. The turtle also turned by 120 degrees at each of the three corners. The total turning was 120 + 120 + 120, or 360 degrees. This is exactly the number of degrees it takes to turn in a complete circle.

Project 5. What would happen if the triangle had longer sides (say five units)? What would happen to the total trip length? How about the total turning angle? Experiment with this until you are convinced that the total turning for a triangle is 360 degrees no matter what the length of the sides is.

Now that we know about triangles, what

about squares? If we keep the side length at
three units, the procedure for a square looks
like this:

```
FORWARD 3
TURN 90
FORWARD 3
TURN 90
FORWARD 3
TURN 90
FORWARD 3
TURN 90
```

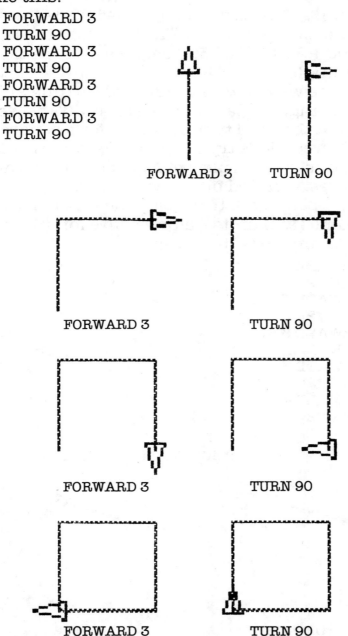

FORWARD 3   TURN 90

FORWARD 3   TURN 90

FORWARD 3   TURN 90

FORWARD 3   TURN 90

Now let's do our calculations again and see what we get. Since the turtle moved three units on each of the four sides, the total path length is 12 units. The turtle also turned 90 degrees four times. Guess what! The total turning is 90 + 90 + 90 + 90, or 360 degrees — the same as for triangles.

Since we know that the total turning angle for a triangular path of any size is 360 degrees, and that the total turning angle for a square is 360 degrees, let's try one more figure to see if this leads us to a rule. Let's pick a path with five sides. A closed figure with five sides is called a *pentagon*. If we keep the side length the same (at 3 units), a procedure for drawing a pentagon looks like this:

```
FORWARD 3
TURN 72
FORWARD 3
TURN 72
FORWARD 3
TURN 72
FORWARD 3
TURN 72
FORWARD 3
TURN 72
```

FORWARD 3   TURN 72

FORWARD 3   TURN 72

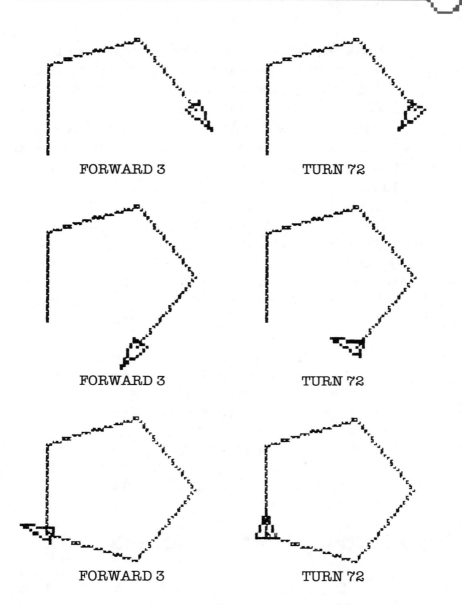

FORWARD 3   TURN 72

FORWARD 3   TURN 72

FORWARD 3   TURN 72

Once again we can do our calculations and
see what we get. The turtle moved three units
on each of the five sides, so the total path length
is 15 units. The turtle also turned 72 degrees
five times. The total turning is 72 + 72 + 72 +
72 + 72, or 360 degrees.

It seems that no matter how many sides our path has, as long as we end up in exactly the same place that we started, we will have turned a total of 360 degrees.

This is pretty useful information since it gives us a way of showing how all simple closed figures are related to each other. The name for this rule is the Turtle Total Trip Theorem — just in case you are interested.

You probably noticed that there was no such rule for the total path length. No matter how long your trip is — say going from home to the library and back — you will have turned 360 degrees if you end up pointing in exactly the same direction in which you started.

Project 6. Can you write a procedure for making a triangle with the same total path length as a pentagon whose sides are three units long? How many units long would each side of the triangle be? Does this show you that you can't tell the shape of a path from knowing its total path length and turning angle?

Some Trips For The Big Trak ...

Now that we know about total turtle trips, let's try some out with the Big Trak. First enter the procedure for a square with a side length of 2 units. (Remember to press the clear button (CLR) before entering this procedure.)

FORWARD 2
TURN 15
FORWARD 2

TURN 15
FORWARD 2
TURN 15
FORWARD 2
TURN 15

   Next press the GO key and watch the Big
Trak move in a square path.

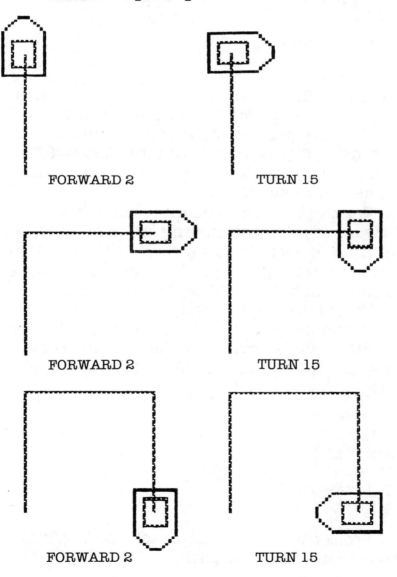

FORWARD 2

TURN 15

FORWARD 2

TURN 15

FORWARD 2

TURN 15

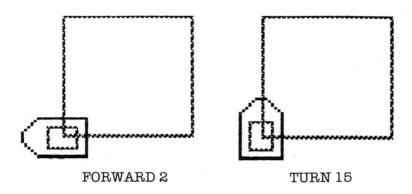

FORWARD 2   TURN 15

If we add up the total trip length you will see that the Big Trak traveled eight units as it went in its square path. If you add up the turning angles, you will find that the Big Trak turned 60 units — the amount needed to turn in one complete circle.

For the Big Trak, the total trip theorem states that the total turning angle must be 60 units. Let's try this out by having the Big Trak move in a triangular path. To draw a triangle we must turn three times. Since the total turning is 60 units, then each of the three turns should be 20 units. To try this out, clear the Big Trak (by pressing the CLR key) and enter the following procedure for a triangular path:

FORWARD 2
TURN 20
FORWARD 2
TURN 20
FORWARD 2
TURN 20

Press the GO key and watch the Big Trak move in a triangular path.

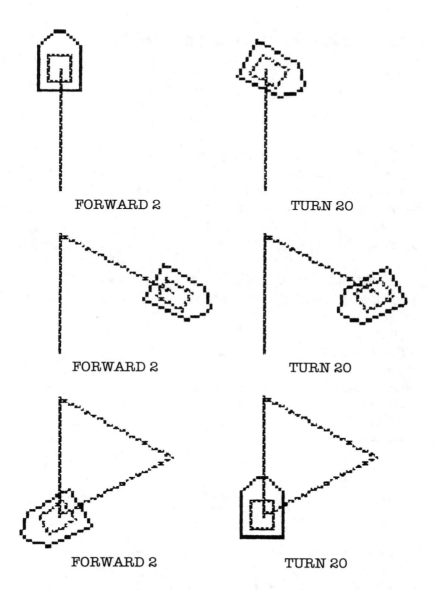

FORWARD 2   TURN 20

FORWARD 2   TURN 20

FORWARD 2   TURN 20

If everything went according to plan, your
Big Trak should have moved in a triangular
path and should be back where it started.

As you can see, the Turtle Total Trip
Theorem is a handy tool for figuring the angles
we need to turn for any number of sides in our
path!

Some Trips For The Turtle Tiles ...

Compared to our turtle or the Big Trak, Turtle Tiles have only a few limited turning angles, but we can still show the total trip theorem with them anyway.

First we can make a procedure for a small square, remembering that if we turn the Turtle Tile by two units it will turn by 90 degrees. Set a tile face up in front of you. Next, use your tiles to follow this procedure:

FORWARD 1
TURN 2
FORWARD 1
TURN 2
FORWARD 1
TURN 2
FORWARD 1
TURN 2

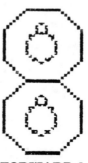

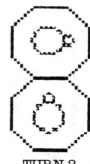

FORWARD 1   TURN 2

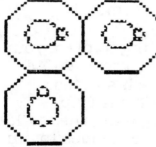

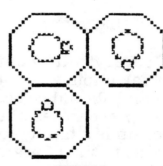

FORWARD 1   TURN 2

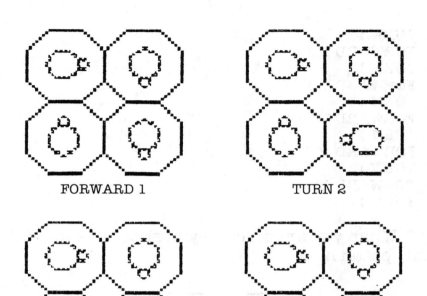

FORWARD 1   TURN 2

FORWARD 1   TURN 2

If we add everything up we see that the total trip length is four units and that the total turning is eight units. Since turning the Turtle Tile by eight units turns it in a circle, this is not surprising.

Suppose we now want to make a Turtle Tile procedure to create a path with eight sides. Since the total turning angle is eight units, then we need to turn one unit for each of the eight sides. Use your Turtle Tiles to follow this procedure:

FORWARD 1
TURN 1
FORWARD 1
TURN 1
FORWARD 1

TURN 1
FORWARD 1
TURN 1
FORWARD 1
TURN 1
FORWARD 1
TURN 1
FORWARD 1
TURN 1
FORWARD 1
TURN 1

When you are all done you should have this pattern.

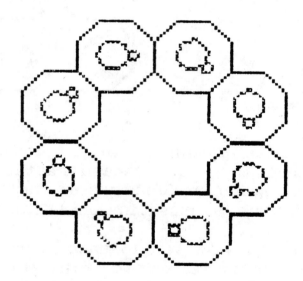

Now that you know all about closed paths, let's look at some paths that don't close completely, no matter how hard we try!

CHAPTER FIVE

You Can't Get There From Here
Paths That Don't Close

Suppose you want to send your robot on a trip where the ending point is different from the starting point. There are many paths you could choose. For example, you could have the turtle move around three sides of a square and then stop. If you wanted to, though, you could close this path by having the turtle travel along the fourth side of the square path.

Did you know that there are some paths that don't close, no matter how hard we try? Impossible? Well, keep reading and you will learn about some very interesting paths.

If you find the material in this chapter to be a bit on the complicated side, you might want to save it for later and move on to the next chapter.

Strange Paths For The Turtle ...

Suppose you want to have the robot go in a triangular path which has two equal sides and has one turning angle of 90 degrees. We can start this path with sides four units long:

    FORWARD 4
    TURN 90
    FORWARD 4

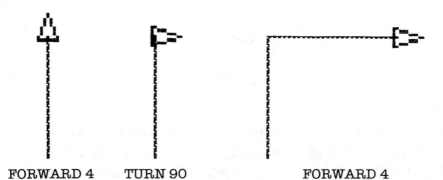

FORWARD 4   TURN 90   FORWARD 4

Next, we need to figure out how much to turn. Since we already turned 90 degrees, and we need to turn by 360 when we are done, we have 270 degrees left to go. For the triangle we are trying to make, we need to turn by two equal amounts, or by 135 degrees each time. Making the first turn is easy:

TURN 135

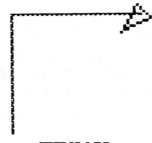

TURN 135

Now comes the tricky part. How far forward should we go? Let's try moving 4 units and see where that leaves us:

FORWARD 4

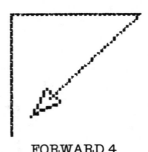

FORWARD 4

Hmmm, that didn't quite make it. We are clearly going in the right direction, but we didn't go far enough. Let's go forward by one

more unit:
FORWARD 1

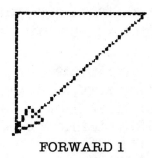

FORWARD 1

We are closer, but we still haven't gotten to our starting point. Let's try going one more unit:
FORWARD 1

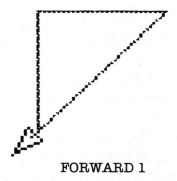

FORWARD 1

Hmmm. Now we have gone past our starting point. The length of this side is larger than five units and smaller than six units. How can this be?

We just sent the turtle on a trip it can't complete! The reason for this is that the third side of our triangular path has a length that is not a whole number of units.

If we could make the turtle take half steps, quarter steps, and so on, we would get very close to our starting point. But if we can only go in lengths made from one unit steps, we will never be able to close this path.

Project 7. If you know about something called a *square root,* you should be able to figure out how long this third side should be. Did you know that no matter how tiny your steps are, you could never get exactly to the starting point? For all practical purposes, though, you could get close enough.

Strange Paths For The Big Trak ...

Making the Big Trak move in paths which don't close isn't too hard — just because of small errors in the turning angle. But let's repeat our triangle experiment with the Big Trak and see how well we do.

First turn on the Big Trak and clear the memory by pressing the CLR key. We will make the first two sides of the triangle two units long. The 90 degree turn is made by turning 15 turning units. Let's enter these three steps and see how we are doing.

```
FORWARD 2
TURN 15
FORWARD 2
```

When you press the GO key the Big Trak should trace out the first two sides of the triangle.

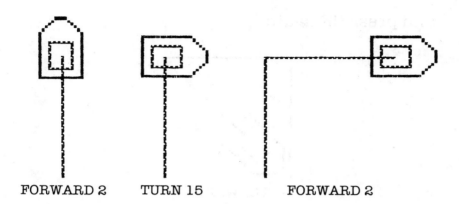

FORWARD 2   TURN 15   FORWARD 2

Next we need to turn the Big Trak by 135 degrees. Since 60 turning units is the same as 360 degrees, we should turn the Big Trak by about 23 units. (Actually, we should turn it by 22 1/2 units, but we can only turn by a whole number of units.) Enter the command:

TURN 23

and press CK so the Big Trak will follow this command.

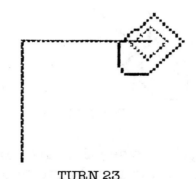

TURN 23

Now our robot is heading back to the place where it started. How far should it go? Let's try going two units. Enter:

FORWARD 2

and press CK again.

FORWARD 2

This didn't take us far enough, but if we enter:

FORWARD 1

and press CK once more, we see that we have gone too far!

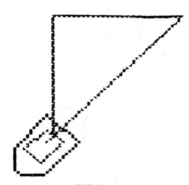

FORWARD 1

Once again we see that we can't close this path if the robot can only move by a whole number of units.

Strange Paths For The Turtle Tiles ...

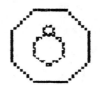

You may not be convinced that this path can't close. After all, just because the Big Trak was not able to complete this path, it doesn't prove anything. As we said before, there are lots of little turning errors that can keep the Big Trak from completing a path exactly.

The Turtle Tiles are much more exact. We will try our strange triangle once more just to prove how strange it really is!

Lay a Turtle Tile on the table in front of you. First make the first two sides of the triangle by following these commands:

FORWARD 2
TURN 2
FORWARD 2

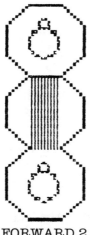

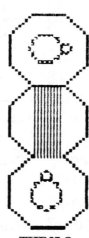

FORWARD 2   TURN 2

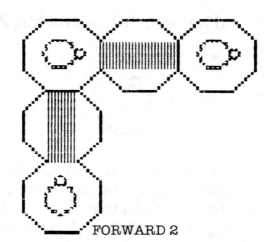

FORWARD 2

Next we need to turn by three units to head back to the starting position:

TURN 3

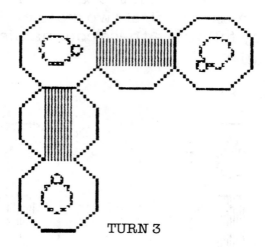

TURN 3

If you next move forward by following the command:

FORWARD 2

you will find that the leading edge of the end tile overlaps the starting tile just a little bit.

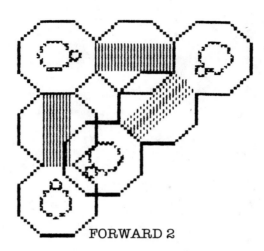

FORWARD 2

This shows that the Turtle Tile version of this triangular path won't close properly either!

There are many interesting pathways you can explore now that you know how to give instructions to the robot turtle. In the next two chapters we will show how the turtle fits into the world of computers, and how to make your Big Trak do some more neat things — such as draw pictures!

CHAPTER SIX

From The Big Trak To The Computer
Your Next Step

The types of commands we have studied so far were designed to let us create pathways for robots. Suppose, instead, that you wanted to use a machine which drew pictures on your TV screen instead of moving in a pathway on the floor. If this special machine could use an imaginary turtle that carried a "pen" in its mouth, then by using commands like FORWARD and TURN we could tell this machine how to draw pictures.

Just think — you would have a machine which follows your commands to draw beautiful pictures on your TV set!

There are machines that do this. They are called *computers.* Many of the inexpensive computers available today even let you display color images. These computers look a bit like typewriters which are connected to the television set. The typewriter keyboard is used to accept commands from you. It is the *input* device — just like the keyboard on the Big Trak. The television screen is the place where the computer draws pictures or types words. It is the *output* device — just like the Big Trak which moves around the floor.

If you had a computer connected to your TV, how would you tell it what to do?

The first thing you would have to do is learn a *computer language,* just as we learned a set of commands for the Big Trak. The job of the computer language is to take your commands and turn them into instructions the computer can follow. There are many computer languages, each made with a special purpose in mind. Since we already know about turtle commands like FORWARD and TURN, it would be best if we could find a computer language which used commands like these.

Fortunately, there are several computer languages which work this way, and new ones seem to be coming all the time. If you can use an Apple computer, you could use languages like SuperPILOT or LOGO. If you use any of the Atari computers, PILOT is the language you want. The Texas Instrument's computer uses the language LOGO for drawing pictures with commands very much like the ones we use with the Big Trak.

While all these languages use turtle commands for drawing pictures, they each have their own special way of doing this. To see how each language operates, let's look at the procedure for drawing a square, ten units on a side, in each of four languages. We will begin with our standard turtle commands.

Turtle

```
FORWARD 10
TURN 90
FORWARD 10
TURN 90
FORWARD 10
TURN 90
FORWARD 10
TURN 90
```

Now let's look at this same procedure written in Atari PILOT.

Atari PILOT

```
GR: DRAW 10
GR: TURN 90
GR: DRAW 10
GR: TURN 90
GR: DRAW 10
```

GR: TURN 90
GR: DRAW 10
GR: TURN 90

The GR: command at the beginning of each line tells PILOT that this is a graphics command. DRAW draws a line on the screen and TURN turns the turtle.

Apple SuperPILOT is very similar to Atari PILOT as shown below.

Apple SuperPILOT

G: D 10
G: S 90
G. D 10
G: S 90
G: D 10
G: S 90
G: D 10
G: S 90

The letter D stands for the draw command, and the letter S is the SuperPILOT turn command (it stands for *spin*).

Next, let's look at LOGO:

LOGO

FORWARD 10
RIGHT 90
FORWARD 10
RIGHT 90
FORWARD 10
RIGHT 90
FORWARD 10
RIGHT 90

As you can see, LOGO is most like the turtle commands we have been using.

Because it is tiring to keep typing the same commands over and over again, these languages have easy ways of doing repeated tasks. The easy way to draw a square in Atari PILOT looks like this:

Atari PILOT

GR: 4(DRAW 10; TURN 90)

This one line command instructs the computer to "Four times draw 10 units and turn 90 degrees." Apple SuperPILOT uses a similar type of command:

Apple SuperPILOT

G: 4(D 10; S 90)

The same commands in LOGO look like this:

LOGO

REPEAT 4
    FORWARD 10
    RIGHT 90

Once you know a little about each language, it is pretty easy to see what is going on.

All of these computer languages let you create many procedures, each with a name of your choosing. The Big Trak can only hold one procedure at a time. If you are using one of the computer languages described above, you can create your own procedures for squares, stars, faces, or anything else you want to draw. All the pictures in this book were drawn by programs using the Atari PILOT turtle commands.

So, as you can see, your experiments with the Big Trak have done much more than teach you about robots. They taught you how to write programs for computers!

Even if you have a computer handy, you should continue to explore the things you can do with your Big Trak. In the next chapter we will show you how to fix up your Big Trak so it will draw pictures as it moves around.

CHAPTER SEVEN

Drawing Pictures
And Other Things To Do
With The Big Trak

How would you like to get your Big Trak to draw pictures? It is easier than you might think. To change the Big Trak so it can draw we need to do two things. First we need a lot of paper (the Big Trak likes to draw BIG pictures). Second, we need to figure out how we can get the Big Trak to hold a pen. Since this is the trickiest part, let's solve that problem first.

To make the Big Trak hold a pen, you will need three items:

1. A felt-tip watercolor pen. (I like the fat ones like those made by Magic Markers or Crayola, but any water color pen will work).

2. A metal U-shaped clamp that fits loosely around the pen. These are called conduit clamps and your hardware store sells them for just a few cents each.

3. Some double-sided sticky foam mounting tape to hold the clamp onto the Big Trak. You can get this tape at most hardware stores and at some drug stores.

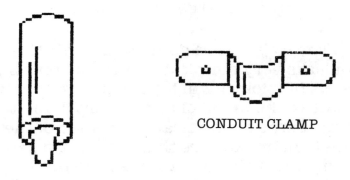

CONDUIT CLAMP

FELT TIPPED PEN

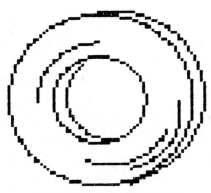

ROLL OF FOAM TAPE

Now that you have all these things, how do you hook them up to the Big Trak? Well, if you look around the sides of the Big Trak you see that it is all pretty bumpy — all except the flat grooved panel at the back side. This is where we will mount our felt-tip pen.

LOCATION FOR THE PEN

The way we are going to mount the pen holder is very simple. We will cut some square pieces of sticky foam tape to put on the flat end pieces of the metal clamp. Before doing this, position the clamp near the center of the back panel and make sure that the felt-tip pen slides down smoothly so that when the Big Trak is set down, the pen tip can touch the floor.

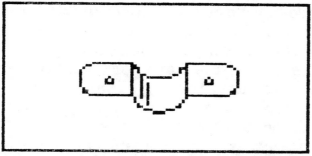

CLAMP POSITION ON BACK OF BIG TRAK

Once you are convinced everything is going to work properly, cut two squares of foam tape, place one square on each flat end of the clamp, and press the clamp in place on the back of the Big Trak. You should now be able to stick the pen into this clamp so its tip will touch the floor. If the pen sticks in the clamp, remove it and add another layer of foam tape to make more room for the pen.

Next, you need paper.

There are many ways to buy large amounts of paper. Your best bet may be to check with your local newspaper to buy what are called "roll ends." A roll end is the paper which is left over at the end of the roll. Usually there is a hundred feet or more of paper that the printer can't use. Most newspapers are happy to sell these roll ends for a dollar or two. You should get the largest width paper you can handle. Paper that is 55" wide is perfect for Big Trak paths. If you can't get newspaper roll ends, you might ask your butcher if he can help you get some wide paper. If all else fails, you can tape sheets of old newspapers together, although this may be more trouble than it is worth.

Once you have fixed up your Big Trak and have your roll of paper, you are ready to let your robot draw some pictures for you. First you must find a nice flat floor with no carpeting on it. Be sure that the ink in the pen you are using can be washed off the floor, in case you have an accident. You must be careful to keep your pens away from carpets and furniture because some watercolor pens can leave permanent stains.

Before taking the cap off the pen, enter the procedure for the path you want to draw. A square with sides two units long fits nicely on 55" wide paper, so you should use short path lengths to make sure the Big Trak doesn't wander off the paper.

After entering your program, set the Big Trak on the paper, take the cap off the pen and slide the pen in the holder so the point rests on the paper surface. As soon as you see the pen resting on the paper, press the GO key. If the pen stays in one place too long, it might make a splotch and soak through the paper. If everything goes according to plan, your Big Trak will draw a picture of its path as it moves along. If the path doesn't quite close, you can make some really pretty pictures by pressing the GO key again and again. Experiment with different pictures. Maybe you can hang some of the prettier ones in your room!

For a different kind of challenge, you can create an obstacle course for the Big Trak to follow. There are lots of ways to make obstacle courses. One way that I like is to buy a piece of wall paneling and use masking tape to make the path I want the Big Trak to follow. You should be able to get a piece of paneling four feet wide by eight feet long from your local lumber yard for a few dollars. Sometimes lumber yards sell old styles or slightly damaged panels for under five dollars. Any panel will work perfectly. Lay the panel on the floor with the smooth back side facing up. Using masking tape, design a path for your Big Trak to follow. Next, see if you can create the procedure for following this path so that it works the first time. This is usually pretty tricky, but it is a lot of fun.

As you can see, there are lots of interesting things you can do with your Big Trak. As you continue to play with it, you will find many applications of your own.

Enjoy yourself!

If you've enjoyed the articles in this book, you'll find the same style and quality in every monthly issue of **COMPUTE!** Magazine. Use this form to order your subscription to **COMPUTE!**

For Fastest Service,
Call Our **Toll-Free** US Order Line
800-334-0868
In NC call 919-275-9809

COMPUTE!
P.O. Box 5406
Greensboro, NC 27403

My Computer Is:
☐ PET ☐ Apple ☐ Atari ☐ OSI ☐ Other _____ ☐ Don't yet have one...

☐ $20.00 One Year US Subscription
☐ $36.00 Two Year US Subscription
☐ $54.00 Three Year US Subscription

Subscription rates outside the US:

☐ $25.00 Canada   F = 2
☐ $38.00 Europe/Air Delivery   Fl = 3
☐ $48.00 Middle East, North Africa, Central America/Air Mail   Fl = 5
☐ $88.00 South America, South Africa, Australasia/Air Mail   Fl = 7
☐ $25.00 International Surface Mail (lengthy, unreliable delivery)   Fl = 4,6,8

Name _____

Address _____

City _____ State _____ Zip _____

Country _____

Payment must be in US Funds drawn on a US Bank; International Money Order, or charge card.

☐ Payment Enclosed   ☐ VISA
☐ MasterCard   ☐ American Express
Acc't. No. _____ Expires ____ / ____

05-1

COMPUTE! Books

P.O. Box 5406   Greensboro, NC 27403

Ask your retailer for these **COMPUTE! Books**. If he or she has sold out, order directly from **COMPUTE!**

For Fastest Service
Call Our **TOLL FREE US Order Line**
800-334-0868
In NC call 919-275-9809

Quantity	Title	Price	Total
_____	**The Beginner's Guide To Buying A Personal Computer** (Add $1.00 shipping and handling. Outside US add $4.00 air mail; $2.00 surface mail.)	$ 3.95	_____
_____	**COMPUTE!'s First Book of Atari** (Add $2.00 shipping and handling. Outside US add $4.00 air mail; $2.00 surface mail.)	$12.95	_____
_____	**Inside Atari DOS** (Add $2.00 shipping and handling. Outside US add $4.00 air mail; $2.00 surface mail.)	$19.95	_____
_____	**COMPUTE!'s First Book of PET/CBM** (Add $2.00 shipping and handling. Outside US add $4.00 air mail; $2.00 surface mail.)	$12.95	_____
_____	**Programming the PET/CBM** (Add $3.00 shipping and handling. Outside US add $9.00 air mail; $3.00 surface mail.)	$24.95	_____
_____	**Every Kid's First Book of Robots and Computers** (Add $1.00 shipping and handling. Outside US add $4.00 air mail; $2.00 surface mail.)	$ 4.95	_____
_____	**COMPUTE!'s Second Book of Atari** (Add $2.00 shipping and handling. Outside US add $4.00 air mail; $2.00 surface mail.)	$12.95	_____
_____	**COMPUTE!'s First Book of VIC** (Add $2.00 shipping and handling. Outside US add $4.00 air mail; $2.00 surface mail.)	$12.95	_____

All orders must be prepaid (money order, check, or charge). All payments must be in US funds. NC residents add 4% sales tax.

☐ Payment enclosed   Please charge my: ☐ VISA   ☐ MasterCard
☐ American Express   Acc't. No. _____ Expires _____ / _____

Name _____

Address _____

City _____ State _____ Zip _____

Country _____

Allow 4-5 weeks for delivery.

05-1